## PLATE I

*'A man of a certain probity and worth, immortal and natural'* (page 157)

# Men of Concord

*and some others* AS PORTRAYED IN THE JOURNAL OF *Henry David Thoreau* EDITED BY FRANCIS H. ALLEN WITH IL-LUSTRATIONS BY N. C. WYETH

HOUGHTON MIFFLIN COMPANY · BOSTON

The Riverside Press Cambridge

1936

The Riverside Press
CAMBRIDGE · MASSACHUSETTS
PRINTED IN THE U.S.A.

# PREFACE

IN THIS volume I have brought together most of the passages in Thoreau's Journal that deal with the men and women he saw and talked with as he went in and out among them in the practice of his two professions of surveyor and saunterer. I have called the book *Men of Concord* because that seemed on the whole a fairly descriptive title, but no reader need be surprised if now and then he encounters a woman in it and if he finds that not all the men are Concordians.

I count myself particularly fortunate in being associated with Mr. Wyeth in carrying out this long-cherished project. His pictures speak for themselves. It is easy to see that they are no mere perfunctory 'illustrations' of Thoreau's text. Besides being a New-Englander by birth and inheritance, Wyeth is a lifelong admirer of Thoreau, whose spirit has become a part of him. His work for this book, therefore, is a tribute from an intellectual disciple to an author who has had an important formative influence on his character and work. I think the reader will feel that through these pictures he himself has come almost into personal contact with Thoreau and with the men of Concord.

Many of the footnotes that appear in this volume are taken, in substance or *verbatim*, from the *Journal of Henry David Thoreau*, Walden Edition (1906). This is done with the approval of the publishers, and I have felt the more at liberty to use them because most if not all of them were originally written by myself as associate editor of the Journal. I have made no systematic attempt to identify all persons named in these extracts: that would have entailed an unwarranted amount of labor on the part of a person who is not so fortunate as to live in Concord. But a consultation of the map compiled by Mr. Herbert W. Gleason for the *Journal* and of the index to its fourteen volumes, which was made under my direction, has enabled me to make certain identifications that may be of interest to some readers. It is unnecessary to explain that 'R. W. E.' stands for 'Ralph Waldo Emerson,' and C., of course, is always William Ellery Channing, the younger, who was Thoreau's most frequent companion on his Concord walks.

F. H. A.

# ILLUSTRATIONS IN COLOR

# INTRODUCTION

MANY readers, thinking of Henry D. Thoreau as the stanch individualist, the apostle of wild nature, the rebel against man-made institutions, the 'hermit of Walden,' forget that he had any but the most formal relations with human beings outside of his own family. And yet his Journal records many and many a conversation with fellow-townsmen, and its readers encounter much shrewd and understanding comment on the ways and manners of this and that individual or group. He talked familiarly with farmers, hunters, and fishermen — as familiarly as he did with his friend Channing, with Edward Hoar, Daniel Ricketson, and H. G. O. Blake.

Dr. Edward Emerson, in his *Henry Thoreau as Remembered by a Young Friend,* has testified to the regard in which Thoreau's humbler neighbors held him. Sam Staples, the tax-collector, constable, and jailer, he says, liked and respected Thoreau and when he arrested him upon his refusal to pay a poll-tax to support a slave-holding government, he said, 'I'll pay your tax, Henry, if you're hard up,' not understanding at first that "twas nothin' but principle' with him.[1] And after speaking of Thoreau's propensity for taking the other side in conversation 'for the joy of the intellectual fencing,' Dr. Emerson goes on to say: 'Thoreau held this trait in check with women and children, and with humble people who were no match for him. With them he was simple, gentle, friendly, and amusing.' 'His simple, direct speech

---

[1] It is interesting to recall the fact that Thoreau's essay on 'Civil Disobedience,' first published in 1849 and containing an account of his short imprisonment in Concord Jail in 1846, was declared by Gandhi to have been one of his chief sources of inspiration in the revolt against British rule in India that stirred the whole world some eighty years afterward.

and look and bearing were such that no plain, common man would put him down in his books as a fool, or visionary, or helpless, as the scholar, writer, or reformer would often be regarded by him. . . . He loved to talk with all kinds and conditions of men if they had no hypocrisy or pretense about them, and though high in his standard of virtue, and most severe with himself, could be charitable to the failings of humble fellow-men.' A man who lived on a farm and had worked in the Thoreaus' plumbago-mill told Dr. Emerson that Thoreau was the best friend he ever had. 'He was always straight in his ways: and was very particular to be agreeable. . . . When I saw him crossing my field I always wanted to go and have a talk with him. . . . He liked to talk as long as you did, and what he said was new.'

'What he said was new.' Thoreau was no mere gossip. In his talks with his neighbors he sought information and he gave it. And, besides that, he met them on their higher levels and brought out the best in them, to their mutual advantage. He asked Therien, the philosophical wood-chopper, 'if he had got a new idea this summer' and received a pertinent answer. Rice tells him the secret of his success-ful life. Barefooted old Brooks Clark shows him how a poor man can be happy. The simple folk perceived Thoreau's genuineness and talked freely with him because they knew he respected them. He was far from sympathetic with the average money-making business man and he hated any form of vulgarity. Of elegant manners and fine clothes he was suspicious, but he met thinking men on their own level and as simply as he met the men who worked with their hands.

There can be no question that Thoreau enjoyed these conversations with the men of Concord for the agreeable human warmth of the contact, but his acquisitive mind always welcomed the opportunities they afforded for adding to his store of information on everything to do with Concord and its natural history, and the Journal contains a vast amount of lore of this kind — much more than the purpose of this book admits of including.

But there were farmers and farmers; and not all of them were agreeable companions. After three days of surveying in December, 1853, he writes: 'All I find is old bound-marks, and the slowness and dullness of farmers reconfirmed. . . . It is remarkable how unprofitable it is for the most part to talk with farmers. They commonly stand on their good behavior and attempt to moralize or philosophize in a serious conversation. Sportsmen and loafers are better company.' And again, in October, 1859, he draws a contrast between the poets' idealized farmer and the farmer struggling under a mortgage, supporting an idiot, and 'carrying through' a decrepit old man whose property he has taken in return for his living and who has lived beyond his time.

But then there were Minott and Rice and the Hosmers and Ebby Hubbard and a number of others with whom Thoreau always enjoyed a 'crack,' to say nothing of the 'sportsmen and loafers,' and there were, besides, the farmers he did not know, whom in some moods, perhaps, he loved best of all!

'How I love [he says] the simple, reserved countrymen, my neighbors, who mind their own business and let me alone; who never waylaid nor shot at me (to my knowledge) when I crossed their fields, though each one has a gun in his house. For nearly twoscore years I have known, at a distance, these long-suffering men, — whom I never spoke to, who never spoke to me, — and now I feel a certain tenderness for them, as if this long probation were but the prelude to an eternal friendship.'

But besides the farmers, the fishermen and hunters, and the literary folk, there was another class of Concordian that interested Thoreau — the Irish. Even before the famine of 1846 there were Irish immigrants in Concord. At the very least there were John Field and his family and Hugh Quoil, the soldier of Waterloo. With the increased immigration that began in 1847 the Irish laborers became a more familiar sight, but they still seemed an alien element in the New England countryside. Thoreau was interested in their old-country ways of doing things, and he liked their simplicity and loyalty, though not blind to the faults of a race that had long been oppressed. The Journal shows more than one act of kindness on his part toward the Concord Irish, and some of the finest bits of writing in it have to do with such persons as Hugh Quoil, John Field, and little Johnny Riordan.

Not a little of the pleasure that Thoreau got from his short excursions to the seashore was derived from his talks with the seafarers and the salt-water fishermen he met with. And finally there were the Indians. It is known that Thoreau planned writing a book about them. He made many notes on his Maine Indian guides and the information he obtained from them, much of which appears in *The Maine Woods*. Only those Indians, however, who were residents, permanent or temporary, of Concord are included in this book.

Concord, to Thoreau, often meant the world. Even to us it means more than just Concord in Middlesex County, Massachusetts. As Boston has been said to be a state of mind, so Concord is a period in history, and this book, I hope, has a certain historical interest aside from the record it presents of Thoreau and his neighbors. It is a sort of cross-section of Concord life in the middle of the nineteenth century. Besides the intellectual life that includes such men as Emerson, Hawthorne, Channing, and the Hoars, we are shown the life of the farmers and farm laborers, the pot-hunters and fishermen, in the days before tractors and trucks and mowing-machines and reapers, when the grass was cut with the scythe, and the mowers slaked their thirst with molasses and ginger and water; when the young cattle were driven to the New Hampshire hill pastures for the summer and back again in the fall; when the farmer's wife blew the horn at noon to call her husband and sons and the hired men home from the fields for dinner; when sawmills and grist-mills on the small streams supplied the neighborhood with lumber and meal and flour; when hunting and fishing brought returns that kept a few of their devotees from starving; when the Irish immigrant was still largely Irish in his outlook; when Concord was Concord.

F. H. A.

# MEN OF CONCORD

## AN OLD ENGLISHMAN

*May 7*, 1838. We occasionally meet an individual of a character and disposition so entirely the reverse of our own that we wonder if he can indeed be another man like ourselves. We doubt if we ever could draw any nearer to him, and understand him. Such was the old English gentleman whom I met with to-day in H.[1] Though I peered in at his eyes I could not discern myself reflected therein. The chief wonder was how we could ever arrive at so fair-seeming an intercourse upon so small ground of sympathy. He walked and fluttered like a strange bird at my side, prying into and making a handle of the least circumstance. The bustle and rapidity of our communication were astonishing; we skated in our conversation. All at once he would stop short in the path, and, in an abstracted air, query whether the steamboat had reached Bath or Portland, addressing me from time to time as his familiar genius, who could understand what was passing in his mind without the necessity of uninterrupted oral communication.

[1] Hallowell, Maine. Thoreau was on a trip of a fortnight into Maine. This was ten years before his first trip to the Maine woods.

## A LEAN FARM

*February* 13, 1841.  My neighbor says that his hill-farm is poor stuff and 'only fit to hold the world together.' He deserves that God should give him better for so brave a treating of his gifts, instead of humbly putting up therewith.  It is a sort of stay, or gore, or gusset, and he will not be blinded by modesty or gratitude, but sees it for what it is; knowing his neighbor's fertile land, he calls his by its right name.  But perhaps my farmer forgets that his lean soil has sharpened his wits.  This is a crop it was good for.  And beside, you see the heavens at a lesser angle from the hill than from the vale.

## THERIEN, THE WOODCHOPPER, AND THE RAILROAD MEN

*July*, 1845.  Here I know I am in good company; here is the world, its centre and metropolis, and all the palms of Asia and the laurels of Greece and the firs of the Arctic Zone incline thither.  Here I can read Homer, if I would have books, as well as in Ionia, and not wish myself in Boston, or New York, or London, or Rome, or Greece.  In such place as this he wrote or sang.  Who should come to my lodge just now but a true Homeric boor, one of those Paphlagonian men?  Alek Therien, he called himself; a Canadian now, a woodchopper, a post-maker; makes fifty posts — holes them, *i.e.* — in a day; and who made his last supper on a woodchuck which his dog caught.  And he too has heard of Homer, and *if it were not for books, would not know what to do* rainy days. Some priest once, who could read glibly from the Greek itself, taught him reading in a measure — his verse, at least, in his turn — away by the Trois Rivières, at Nicolet. And now I must read to him, while he holds the book, Achilles' reproof of Patroclus on his sad countenance. . . .

He has a neat bundle of white oak bark under his arm for a sick man, gathered this Sunday morning. 'I suppose there's no harm in going after such a thing to-day.' The simple man. May the gods send him many woodchucks.

And earlier to-day came five Lestrigones, railroad men who take care of the road, some of them at least. They still represent the bodies of men, transmitting arms and legs and bowels downward from those remote days to more remote. They have some got a rude wisdom withal, thanks to their dear experience. And one with them, a handsome younger man, a sailor-like, Greek-like man, says: 'Sir, I like your notions. I think I shall live so myself. Only I should like a wilder country, where there is more game. I have been among the Indians near Appalachicola. I have lived with them. I like your kind of life. Good day. I wish you success and happiness.'

Therien said this morning (July 16th, Wednesday), 'If those beans were mine, I shouldn't like to hoe them till the dew was off.' He was going to his woodchopping. 'Ah!' said I, 'that is one of the notions the farmers have got, but I don't believe it.' 'How thick the pigeons are!' said he. 'If working every day were not my trade, I could get all the meat I should want by hunting, — pigeons, woodchucks, rabbits, partridges, — by George! I could get all I should want for a week in one day.'

JOHN FIELD

*August* 23, 1845.  I set out this afternoon to go a-fishing for
pickerel to eke out my scanty fare of vegetables.  From
Walden I went through the woods to Fair Haven, but by
the way the rain came on again, and my fates compelled
me to stand a half-hour under a pine, piling boughs over my
head, and wearing my pocket handkerchief for an umbrella;
and when at length I had made one cast over the pickerel-
weed, the thunder gan romblen in the heven with that grisly
steven that Chaucer tells of.  (The gods must be proud,
with such forked flashes and such artillery to rout a poor
unarmed fisherman.)  I made haste to the nearest hut for a
shelter.  This stood a half a mile off the road, and so much
the nearer to the pond.  There dwelt a shiftless Irishman,
John Field, and his wife, and many children, from the broad-
faced boy that ran by his father's side to escape the rain to
the wrinkled and sibyl-like, crone-like infant, not knowing
whether to take the part of age or infancy, that sat upon its
father's knee as in the palaces of nobles, and looked out from
its home in the midst of wet and hunger inquisitively upon
the stranger, with the privilege of infancy; the young creature not knowing but it might be the last of a line of kings
instead of John Field's poor starveling brat, or, I should
rather say, still knowing that it was the last of a noble line
and the hope and cynosure of the world.  An honest, hard-
working, but shiftless man plainly was John Field; and his
wife, she too was brave to cook so many succeeding dinners
in the recesses of that lofty stove; with round, greasy face
and bare breast, still thinking to improve her condition one
day; with the never absent mop in hand, and yet no effects
of it visible anywhere.  The chickens, like members of the

family, stalked about the room, too much humanized to roast well. They stood and looked in my eye or pecked at my shoe. He told me his story, how hard he worked bogging for a neighbor, at ten dollars an acre and the use of the land with manure for one year, and the little broad-faced son worked cheerfully at his father's side the while, not knowing, alas! how poor a bargain he had made. Living, John Field, alas! without arithmetic; failing to live.

'Do you ever fish?' said I. 'Oh yes, I catch a mess when I am lying by; good perch I catch.' 'What's your bait?' 'I catch shiners with fishworms, and bait the perch with them.' 'You'd better go now, John,' said his wife, with glistening, hopeful face. But poor John Field disturbed but a couple of fins, while I was catching a fair string, and he said it was his luck; and when he changed seats luck changed seats too. Thinking to live by some derivative old-country mode in this primitive new country, *e.g.* to catch perch with shiners.

### A LOST HOUND

1845–46. 'Have you seen my hound, sir? I want to know — what! a lawyer's office? law books? — if you've seen anything of a hound about here. Why, what do you do here?' 'I live here. No, I haven't.' 'Haven't you heard one in the woods anywhere?' 'Oh, yes, I heard one this evening.' 'What do you do here?' 'But he was some way off.' 'Which side did he seem to be?' 'Well, I should think he was the other side of the pond.' 'This is a large dog; makes a large track. He's been out hunting from Lexington for a week. How long have you lived here?' 'Oh, about a year.' 'Somebody said there was a man up here had a camp in the woods somewhere, and he'd got him.' 'Well, I don't know of any-body. There's Britton's camp over on the other road. It may be there.' 'Isn't there anybody in these woods?' 'Yes, they are chopping right up here behind me.' 'How far is it?' 'Only a few steps. Hark a moment. There, don't you hear the sound of their axes?'

### THERIEN AND THE CHICKADEES

Therien, the woodchopper, was here yesterday, and while I was cutting wood, some chickadees hopped near pecking the bark and chips and the potato-skins I had thrown out. 'What do you call them,' he asked. I told him.

'What do *you* call them,' asked I. '*Mezezence* [?],' [1] I think he said. 'When I eat my dinner in the woods,' said he, 'sitting very still, having kindled a fire to warm my coffee, they come and light on my arm and peck at the potato in my fingers. I like to have the little fellers about me.' Just then one flew up from the snow and perched on the wood I was holding in my arms, and pecked it, and looked me familiarly in the face. *Chicadee-dee-dee-dee-dee*, while others were whistling phebe, — *phe-bee*, — in the woods behind the house.

[1] Probably *mésange*, the French for 'titmouse,' which is applied by the French Canadians to the chickadee, a species of titmouse.

THOMAS CARLYLE

1845–47.   Carlyle told R. W. E. that he first discovered that he was not a jackass on reading 'Tristram Shandy' and Rousseau's 'Confessions,' especially the last.  His first essay is an article in *Fraser's Magazine* on two boys quarrelling.

HUGH QUOIL, THE SOLDIER OF WATERLOO *to give for no purpose for his life*

1845–47.   I had one neighbor within half a mile for a short time when I first went to the woods, Hugh Quoil, an Irishman who had been a soldier at Waterloo, Colonel Quoil, as he was called, — I believe that he had killed a colonel and ridden off his horse, — who lived from hand — sometimes to mouth, — though it was commonly a glass of rum that the hand carried.  He and his wife awaited their fate together in an old ruin in Walden woods.  What life he got — or what means of death — he got by ditching.

I never was much acquainted with Hugh Quoil, though sometimes I met him in the path, and now do believe that a solid shank-bone, and skull which no longer aches, lie somewhere, and can still be produced, which once with garment of flesh and broadcloth were called and hired to do work as Hugh Quoil.  He was a man of manners and gentlemanlike, as one who had seen the world, and was capable of more civil speech than you could well attend to.  At a distance he had seemingly a ruddy face as of biting January, but nearer at hand it was bright carmine.  It would have burnt your finger to touch his cheek.  He wore a straight-bodied snuff-colored coat which had long been familiar with him, and carried a turf-knife in his hand — instead of a sword. He had fought on the English side before, but he fought on the Napoleon side now. Napoleon went to St. Helena; Hugh Quoil came to Walden Pond. I heard that he used to tell travellers who inquired about myself that —— and Thoreau owned the *farm* together, but Thoreau lived on the *place* and carried it on.

He was thirstier than I, and drank more, probably, but not out of the pond. That was never the lower for him. Perhaps I ate more than he. The last time I met him, the only time I spoke with him, was at the foot of the hill on the highway as I was crossing to the spring one summer afternoon, the pond water being too warm for me. I was crossing the road with a pail in my hand, when Quoil came

down the hill, wearing his snuff-colored coat, as if it were winter, and shaking with delirium tremens. I hailed him and told him that my errand was to get water at a spring close by, only at the foot of the hill over the fence. He answered, with stuttering and parched lips, bloodshot eye, and staggering gesture, he'd like to see it. 'Follow me there, then.' But I had got my pail full and back before he scaled the fence. And he, drawing his coat about him, to warm him, or to cool him, answered in delirium-tremens, hydrophobia dialect, which is not easy to be written here, he'd heard of it, but had never seen it; and so shivered his way along to town, — to liquor and to oblivion.

On Sundays, brother Irishmen and others, who had gone far astray from steady habits and the village, crossed my bean-field with empty jugs toward Quoil's. But what for? Did they sell rum there? I asked. 'Respectable people they,' 'Know no harm of them,' 'Never heard that they drank too much,' was the answer of all wayfarers. They went by sober, stealthy, silent, skulking (no harm to get elm bark Sundays); returned loquacious, sociable, having long intended to call on you.

At length one afternoon Hugh Quoil, feeling better, perchance, with snuff-colored coat, as usual, paced solitary and soldier-like, thinking of Waterloo, along the woodland road to the foot of the hill by the spring; and there the Fates met him, and threw him down in his snuff-colored coat on the gravel, and got ready to cut his thread; but not till travellers passed, who would raise him up, get him perpendicular, then settle, settle quick; but legs, what are they? 'Lay me down,' says Hugh hoarsely. 'House locked up — key — in pocket — wife in town.' And the Fates cut, and there he lay by the wayside, five feet ten, and looking taller than in life.

He has gone away; his house here 'all tore to pieces.' What kind of fighting or ditching work he finds to do now, how it fares with him, whether his thirst is quenched, whether there is still some semblance of that carmine cheek, struggles still with some liquid demon — perchance on more equal terms — till he swallow him completely, I cannot by any means learn. What his salutation is now, what his January-morning face, what he thinks of Waterloo, what start he has gained or lost, what work still for the ditcher and forester and soldier now, there is no evidence. He was here, the likes of him, for a season, standing light in his shoes like a faded gentleman, with gesture almost learned in drawing-rooms; wore clothes, hat, shoes, cut ditches, felled wood, did farm work for various people, kindled fires, worked enough, ate enough, drank too much. He was one of those unnamed, countless sects of philosophers who founded no school.

Now that he was gone, and his wife was gone too, — for she could not support the solitude, — before it was too late and the house was torn down, I went over to make a call. Now that Irishmen with jugs avoided the old house, I visited it, — an 'unlucky castle now,' said they. There lay his old clothes curled up by habit, as if it were himself, upon his raised plank bed. His pipe lay broken on the hearth; and scattered about were soiled cards — king of diamonds, hearts, spades — on the floor. One black chicken, which they could not catch, still went to roost in the next apartment, stepping silent over the floor, frightened by the sound of its own wings, black as night and as silent, too, not even croaking; awaiting Reynard, its god actually dead. There was the dim outline of a garden which had been planted, but had never received its first hoeing, now over-run with weeds, with burs and cockles, which stick to your clothes; as if in the spring he had contemplated a harvest of corn and beans before that strange trembling of the limbs overtook him. Skin of woodchuck fresh-stretched, never to be cured, met once in bean-field by the Waterloo man with uplifted hoe; no cap, no mittens wanted. Pipe on hearth no more to be lighted, best buried with him.

### EMERSON AND ALCOTT

1845-47. Emerson again is a critic, poet, philosopher, with talent not so conspicuous, not so adequate to his task; but his field is still higher, his task more arduous.[1] Lives a far more intense life; seeks to realize a divine life; his affections and intellect equally developed. Has advanced farther, and a new heaven opens to him. Love and Friendship, Religion, Poetry, the Holy are familiar to him. The life of an Artist;

[1] The comparison is apparently with Carlyle.

more variegated, more observing, finer perception; not so robust, elastic; practical enough in his own field; faithful, a judge of men. There is no such general critic of men and things, no such trustworthy and faithful man. More of the divine realized in him than in any. A poetic critic, reserving the unqualified nouns for the gods.

Alcott is a geometer, a visionary, the Laplace of ethics, more intellect, less of the affections, sight beyond talents, a substratum of practical skill and knowledge unquestionable, but overlaid and concealed by a faith in the unseen and impracticable. Seeks to realize an entire life; a catholic observer; habitually takes in the farthest star and nebula into his scheme. Will be the last man to be disappointed as the ages revolve. His attitude is one of greater faith and expectation than that of any man I know; with little to show; with undue share, for a philosopher, of the weaknesses of humanity. The most hospitable intellect, embracing high and low. For children how much that means, for the insane and vagabond, for the poet and scholar!

Emerson has special talents unequalled. The divine in man has had no more easy, methodically distinct expression. His personal influence upon young persons greater than any man's. In his world every man would be a poet, Love would reign, Beauty would take place, Man and Nature would harmonize.

When Alcott's day comes, laws unsuspected by most will take effect, the system will crystallize according to them, all seals and falsehood will slough off, everything will be in its place.

Emerson does not consider things in respect to their essential utility, but an important partial and relative one, as works of art perhaps. His probes pass one side of their centre of gravity. His exaggeration is of a part, not of the whole.

### CATTLE-DRIVING

I sometimes see a neighbor or two united with their boys and hired men to drive their cattle to some far-off country pasture, fifty or sixty miles distant in New Hampshire, early in the morning, with their sticks and dogs. It is a memorable time with the farmers' boys, and frequently their first journey from home. The herdsman in some mountain pasture is expecting them. And then in the fall, when they go up to drive them back, they speculate as to whether Janet or Brindle will know them. I heard such a boy exclaim on such an occasion, when the calf of the spring returned a heifer, as he stroked her side, 'She knows me, father; she knows me.'

### SETTING FIRE TO THE WOODS

1850.[1] I once set fire to the woods. Having set out, one April day, to go to the sources of Concord River in a boat with a single companion, meaning to camp on the bank at night or seek a lodging in some neighboring country inn or farmhouse, we took fishing tackle with us that we might fitly procure our food from the stream, Indian-like. At the shoemaker's near the river, we obtained a match, which we had forgotten. Though it was thus early in the spring, the

[1] Most of the Journal entries for 1850 bear no precise date.

river was low, for there had not been much rain, and we succeeded in catching a mess of fish sufficient for our dinner
before we had left the town, and by the shores of Fair
Haven Pond we proceeded to cook them. The earth was un-
commonly dry, and our fire, kindled far from the woods in
a sunny recess in the hillside on the east of the pond, suddenly caught the dry grass of the previous year which grew
about the stump on which it was kindled. We sprang to
extinguish it at first with our hands and feet, and then we
fought it with a board obtained from the boat, but in a few
minutes it was beyond our reach; being on the side of a hill,
it spread rapidly upward, through the long, dry, wiry grass
interspersed with bushes.

'Well, where will this end?' asked my companion. I saw
that it might be bounded by Well Meadow Brook on one
side, but would, perchance, go to the village side of the brook.
'It will go to town,' I answered. While my companion
took the boat back down the river, I set out through the
woods to inform the owners and to raise the town. The fire
had already spread a dozen rods on every side and went
leaping and crackling wildly and irreclaimably toward the
wood. That way went the flames with wild delight, and we
felt that we had no control over the demonic creature to
which we had given birth. We had kindled many fires in
the woods before, burning a clear space in the grass, without
ever kindling such a fire as this.

As I ran toward the town through the woods, I could
see the smoke over the woods behind me marking the spot
and the progress of the flames. The first farmer whom I
met driving a team, after leaving the woods, inquired the
cause of the smoke. I told him. 'Well,' said he, 'it is none of
my stuff,' and drove along. The next I met was the owner
in his field, with whom I returned at once to the woods,
running all the way. I had already run two miles. When

# PLATE II

*Thoreau Fishing*

at length we got into the neighborhood of the flames, we met a carpenter who had been hewing timber, an infirm man who had been driven off by the fire, fleeing with his axe. The farmer returned to hasten more assistance. I, who was spent with running, remained. What could I do alone against a front of flame half a mile wide?

I walked slowly through the wood to Fair Haven Cliff, climbed to the highest rock, and sat down upon it to observe the progress of the flames, which were rapidly approaching me, now about a mile distant from the spot where the fire was kindled. Presently I heard the sound of the distant bell giving the alarm, and I knew that the town was on its way to the scene. Hitherto I had felt like a guilty person, — nothing but shame and regret. But now I settled the matter with myself shortly. I said to myself: 'Who are these men who are said to be the owners of these woods, and how am I related to them? I have set fire to the forest, but I have done no wrong therein, and now it is as if the lightning had done it. These flames are but consuming their natural food.' (It has never troubled me from that day to this more than if the lightning had done it. The trivial fishing was all that disturbed me and disturbs me still.) So shortly I settled it with myself and stood to watch the approaching flames. It was a glorious spectacle, and I was the only one there to enjoy it. The fire now reached the base of the cliff and then rushed up its sides. The squirrels ran before it in blind haste, and three pigeons dashed into the midst of the smoke. The flames flashed up the pines to their tops, as if they were powder.

When I found I was about to be surrounded by the fire, I retreated and joined the forces now arriving from the town. It took us several hours to surround the flames with our hoes and shovels and by back fires subdue them. In the midst of all I saw the farmer whom I first met, who had turned indifferently away saying it was none of his stuff, striving earnestly to save his corded wood, his stuff, which the fire had already seized and which it after all consumed.

It burned over a hundred acres or more and destroyed much young wood. When I returned home late in the day, with others of my townsmen, I could not help noticing that the crowd who were so ready to condemn the individual who had kindled the fire did not sympathize with the owners of the wood, but were in fact highly elate and as it were thankful for the opportunity which had afforded them so much sport; and it was only half a dozen owners, so called, though not all of them, who looked sour or grieved, and I felt that I had a deeper interest in the woods, knew them better and should feel their loss more, than any or all of them. The  farmer whom I had first conducted to the woods was obliged to ask me the shortest way back, through his own lot. Why, then, should the half-dozen owners and the individuals who set the fire alone feel sorrow for the loss of the wood, while the rest of the town have their spirits raised? Some of the owners, however, bore their loss like men, but other some declared behind my back that I was a 'damned rascal;' and a flibbertigibbet or two, who crowed like the old cock, shouted some reminiscences of 'burnt woods' from safe recesses for some years after. I have had nothing to say to any of them. The locomotive engine has since burned over nearly all the same ground and more, and in some measure blotted out the memory of the previous fire. For a long time after I had learned this lesson I marvelled that while matches and tinder were contemporaries the world was not consumed; why the houses that have hearths were not burned before another day; if the flames were not as hungry now as when I waked them. I at once ceased to regard the owners and my own fault, — if fault there was any in the matter, — and attended to the phenomenon before me, determined to make the most of it. To be sure, I felt a little ashamed when I reflected on what a trivial occasion this had happened, that at the time I was no better employed than my townsmen.

That night I watched the fire, where some stumps still flamed at midnight in the midst of the blackened waste, wandering through the woods by myself; and far in the night I threaded my way to the spot where the fire had taken, and discovered the now broiled fish, — which had been dressed, — scattered over the burnt grass.

## A BURNER OF BRUSH

*June* 4, 1850. To-day, June 4th, I have been tending a burning in the woods. Ray was there. It is a pleasant fact that you will know no man long, however low in the social scale, however poor, miserable, intemperate, and worthless he may appear to be, a mere burden to society, but you will find at last that there is something which he understands and can do better than any other. I was pleased to hear that one man had sent Ray as the one who had had the most experience in setting fires of any man in Lincoln. He had experience and skill as a burner of brush.

## RUNNING TO A FIRE

*June* 4, 1850. Men go to a fire for entertainment. When I see how eagerly men will run to a fire, whether in warm or in cold weather, by day or by night, dragging an engine at

their heels, I am astonished to perceive how good a purpose the love of excitement is made to serve. What other
force, pray, what offered pay, what disinterested neighbor-
liness could ever effect so much? No, these are boys who are
to be dealt with, and these are the motives that prevail.
There is no old man or woman dropping into the grave but
covets excitement.

### INDIANS IN CONCORD

1850. The names of those who bought these fields of the red
men, the wild men of the woods, are Buttrick, Davis, Barrett, Bulkley, etc., etc. (*Vide* History.) Here and there still
you will find a man with Indian blood in his veins, an eccentric farmer descended from an Indian chief; or you will
see a solitary pure-blooded Indian, looking as wild as ever
among the pines, one of the last of the Massachusetts tribes,
stepping into a railroad car with his gun.

Still here and there an Indian squaw with her dog, her
only companion, lives in some lone house, insulted by school-
children, making baskets and picking berries her employment. You will meet her on the highway, with few children
or none, with melancholy face, history, destiny; stepping
after her race; who had stayed to tuck them up in their
long sleep. For whom berries condescend to grow. I have
not seen one on the Musketaquid for many a year, and some
who came up in their canoes and camped on its banks a
dozen years ago had to ask me where it came from. A lone
Indian woman without children, accompanied by her dog,
wearing the shroud of her race, performing the last offices
for her departed race. Not yet absorbed into the elements

again; a daughter of the soil; one of the nobility of the land. The white man an imported weed, — burdock and mullein, which displace the ground-nut.

### A DRUNKEN DUTCHMAN

1850. Getting into Patchogue [1] late one night in an oyster-boat, there was a drunken Dutchman aboard whose wit reminded me of Shakespeare. When we came to leave the beach, our boat was aground, and we were detained three

[1] On Long Island, New York. It is across Great South Bay from Fire Island, where Thoreau went in July, 1850, to help in the search for the remains of Margaret Fuller, wrecked with her husband and child on her return from Italy.

hours waiting for the tide. In the meanwhile two of the fishermen took an extra dram at the beach house. Then they stretched themselves on the seaweed by the shore in the sun to sleep off the effects of their debauch. One was an inconceivably broadfaced young Dutchman, — but oh! of such a peculiar breadth and heavy look, I should not know whether to call it more ridiculous or sublime. You would say that he had humbled himself so much that he was beginning to be exalted. An indescribable mynheerish stupidity. I was less disgusted by their filthiness and vulgarity, because I was compelled to look on them as animals, as swine in their sty. For the whole voyage they lay flat on their backs on the bottom of the boat, in the bilge-water and wet with each bailing, half insensible and wallowing in their vomit. But ever and anon, when aroused by the rude kicks or curses of the skipper, the Dutchman, who never lost his wit nor equanimity, though snoring and rolling in the vomit produced by his debauch, blurted forth some happy repartee like an illuminated swine. It was the earthiest, slimiest wit I ever heard. The countenance was one of a million. It was unmistakable Dutch. In the midst of a million faces of other races it could not be mistaken. It told of Amsterdam. I kept racking my brains to conceive how he could have been born in America, how lonely he must feel, what he did for fellowship. When we were groping up the narrow creek of Patchogue at ten o'clock at night, keeping our boat off, now from this bank, now from that, with a pole, the two inebriates roused themselves betimes. For in spite of their low estate they seemed to have all their wits as much about them as ever, aye, and all the self-respect they ever had. And the Dutchman gave wise directions to the steerer, which were not heeded. Suddenly rousing himself up where the sharpest-eyed might be bewildered in the darkness, he leaned over the side of the boat and pointed straight down into the creek, averring that that identical hole was a first-rate place for eels. And again he roused himself at the right time and declared what luck he had once had with his pots (not his cups) in another place, which we were floating over in the dark. At last he suddenly stepped on to another boat which was moored to the shore, with a divine ease and sureness, saying, 'Well, good-night, take care of yourselves, I can't be with you any longer.' He was one of the few remarkable men whom I have met. I have been impressed by one or two men in their cups. There was really a divinity stirred within them, so that in their case I have reverenced the drunken, as savages the insane, man. So stupid that he could never be intoxicated. When I said, 'You have had a hard time of it to-day,' he answered with indescribable good humor out of the very midst of his debauch, with watery eyes, 'Well, it doesn't happen every day.' It was happening then. He had taken me aboard on his back, the boat lying a rod from the shore, before I knew his condition. In the darkness our skipper steered with a pole on the bottom, for an oysterman knows the bottom of his bay as well as the shores, and can tell where he is by the soundings.

### AN IRISHMAN'S DEVICE

1850. An Irishman told me that he held up one leg and if he could bring his toe in a range with his eye and the opposite bank he knew that he could jump it. Why, I told him, I can blot out a star with my toe, but I would not engage to jump the distance. It then appeared that he knew when he had got his leg at the right height by a certain hitch

there was in it. I suggested that he should connect his two
ankles with a string.

## SURVEYING

1850. There was a cross-eyed fellow used to help me survey,
— he was my stake-driver, — and all he said was, at every
stake he drove, 'There, I shouldn't like to undertake to
pull *that* up with my teeth.'

## BORROWING A HORSE AND CART

1850. One of my neighbors, of whom I borrowed a horse,
cart, and harness to-day, which last was in a singularly di-
lapidated condition, considering that he is a wealthy farmer,
did not know but I would make a book about it.

## LONG ISLAND OYSTERMEN

*pidity?*

1850. The oystermen had anchored their boat near the
shore without regard to the state of the tide, and when we
came to it to set sail, just after noon, we found that it was
aground. Seeing that they were preparing to push it off, I
was about to take off my shoes and stockings in order to
wade to it first, but a Dutch sailor with a singular bullfrog

or trilobite expression of the eyes, whose eyes were like frog ponds in the broad platter of his cheeks and gleamed like a pool covered with frog-spittle, immediately offered me the use of his back. So mounting, with my legs under his arms, and hugging him like one of the family, he set me aboard of the periauger.

They then leaned their hardest against the stern, bracing their feet against the sandy bottom in two feet of water, the Dutchman with his broad back among them. In the most Dutch-like and easy way they applied themselves to this labor, while the skipper tried to raise the bows, never jerking or hustling but silently exerting what vigor was inherent in them, doing, no doubt, their utmost endeavor, while I pushed with a spike pole; but it was all in vain. It was decided to be unsuccessful; we did not disturb its bed by a grain of sand. 'Well, what now?' said I. 'How long have we got to wait?' 'Till the tide rises,' said the captain. But no man knew of the tide, how it was. So I went in to bathe, looking out for sharks and chasing crabs, and the Dutchman waded out among the mussels to spear a crab. The skipper stuck a clamshell into the sand at the water's edge to discover if it was rising, and the sailors, — the Dutchman and the other, — having got more drink at Oakes's, stretched themselves on the seaweed close to the water's edge and went to sleep. After an hour or more we could discover no change in the shell even by a hair's breadth, from which we learned that it was about the turn of the tide and we must wait some hours longer.

## A BODY ON THE BEACH

1850. I once went in search of the relics of a human body
— a week after a wreck — which had been cast up the day
before on to the beach, though the sharks had stripped off
the flesh. I got the direction from a lighthouse. I should
find it a mile or two distant over the sand, a dozen rods from
the water, by a stick which was stuck up covered with a
cloth. Pursuing the direction pointed out, I expected that I
should have to look very narrowly at the sand to find so
small an object, but so completely smooth and bare was the
beach — half a mile wide of sand — and so magnifying the
mirage toward the sea that when I was half a mile distant
the insignificant stick or sliver which marked the spot looked
like a broken mast in the sand. As if there was no other
object, this trifling sliver had puffed itself up to the vision
to fill the void; and there lay the relics in a certain state,
rendered perfectly inoffensive to both bodily and spiritual
eye by the surrounding scenery, — a slight inequality in the
sweep of the shore. Alone with the sea and the beach, attending to the sea, whose hollow roar seemed addressed to
the ears of the departed, — articulate speech to them. It
was as conspicuous on that sandy plain as if a generation
had labored to pile up a cairn there. Where there were so
few objects, the least was obvious as a mausoleum. It reigned
over the shore. That dead body possessed the shore as no
living one could. It showed a title to the sands which no
living ruler could.

### INDIAN BEGGING

1850. A squaw came to our door to-day with two pap-
pooses, and said, 'Me want a pie.' Theirs is not common
begging. You are merely the rich Indian who shares his
goods with the poor. They merely offer you an opportunity
to be generous and hospitable.

*on a higher level to*

### USED TO DRINKING

*May* 1, 1851. The forenoon that I moved to my house, a
poor old lame fellow [1] who had formerly frozen his feet hob-
bled off the road, came and stood before my door with one
hand on each door-post, looking into the house, and asked
for a drink of water. I knew that rum or something like
it was the only drink he loved, but I gave him a dish of warm
pond water, which was all I had, nevertheless, which to my
astonishment he drank, being used to drinking.

### A SUMMER EVENING

*June* 14, 1851. Met a man driving home his cow from
pasture and stopping to chat with his neighbor; then a boy,
who had set down his pail in the road to stone a bird most
perseveringly, whom I heard afterward behind me telling

[1] Probably Bill Wheeler. See pages 61–63.

his pail to be quiet in a tone of assumed anger, because it squeaked under his arm. . . .

Now I meet an acquaintance coming from a remote field in his hay-rigging, with a jag of wood; who reins up to show me how large a woodchuck he has killed, which he found eating his clover. But now he must drive on, for behind comes a boy taking up the whole road with a huge roller drawn by a horse, which goes lumbering and bouncing along, getting out of the way of night, — while the sun has gone the other way, — and making such a noise as if it had the contents of a tinker's shop in its bowels, and rolls the whole road smooth like a newly sown grain-field.

## IRISH FARMING IN NEW ENGLAND

*June* 29, 1851. I am interested to observe how old-country methods of farming resources are introduced among us. The Irish laborer, for instance, seeing that his employer is contemplating some agricultural enterprise, as ditching or fencing, suggests some old-country mode with which he has been familiar from a boy, which is often found to be cheaper as well as more ornamental than the common; and Patrick is allowed to accomplish the object his own way, and for once exhibits some skill and has not to be shown, but, working with a will as well as with pride, does better than ever in the old country. Even the Irishman exhibits what might be mistaken for a Yankee knack, exercising a merely inbred skill derived from the long teachings and practice of his ancestors.

I saw an Irishman building a bank of sod where his employer had contemplated building a bank wall, piling up very neatly and solidly with his spade and a line the sods taken from the rear, and coping the face at a very small angle from the perpendicular, intermingling the sods with bushes as they came to hand, which would grow and strengthen the whole. It was much more agreeable to the eye, as well as less expensive, than stone would have been, and he thought that it would be equally effective as a fence and no less durable. But it is true only experience will show when the same practice may be followed in this climate and in Ireland, — whether our atmosphere is not too dry to admit of it. At any rate it was wise in the farmer thus to avail himself of any peculiar experience which his hired laborer possessed. That was what he *should* buy.

## SAM, THE JAILER

*July* 6, 1851. There is some advantage in being the humblest, cheapest, least dignified man in the village, so that the very stable boys shall damn you. Methinks I enjoy that advantage to an unusual extent. There is many a coarsely well-meaning fellow, who knows only the skin of me, who addresses me familiarly by my Christian name. I get the whole good of him and lose nothing myself. There is 'Sam,' the jailer, — whom I never call Sam, however, — who exclaimed last evening: 'Thoreau, are you going up the street pretty soon? Well, just take a couple of these handbills along and drop one in at Hoar's piazza and one at Holbrook's, and I'll do as much for you another time.' I am not above being used, aye abused, sometimes.

## PEREZ BLOOD AND HIS TELESCOPE

*July* 7, 1851. I have been to-night with Anthony Wright to look through Perez Blood's telescope a second time. A dozen of Blood's neighbors were swept along in the stream of our curiosity. One who lived half a mile this side said that Blood had been down that way within a day or two with his terrestrial, or day, glass, looking into the eastern horizon at the hills of Billerica, Burlington, and Woburn. I was amused to see what sort of respect this man with a telescope had obtained from his neighbors, something akin to that which savages award to civilized men, though in this case the interval between the parties was very slight. Mr. Blood, with his skull-cap on, his short figure, his north European figure, made me think of Tycho Brahe. He did not invite us into his house this cool evening, — men nor women, — nor did he ever before to my knowledge. I am still contented to see the stars with my naked eye. Mr. Wright asked him what his instrument cost. He answered, 'Well, that is something I don't like to tell.' (Stuttering or hesitating in his speech a little as usual.) 'It is a very proper question, however.' 'Yes,' said I, 'and you think that you have given a very proper answer.'

BOVINE APPETITES

*July* 14, 1851. Passing over the Great Fields (where I have been surveying a road) this forenoon, where were some early turnips, the county commissioners plucked and pared them with their knives and ate them. I, too, tried hard to chew a mouthful of raw turnip and realize the life of cows and oxen, for it might be a useful habit in extremities. These things occur as the seasons revolve. These are things which travellers will do. How many men have tasted a raw turnip! How few have eaten a whole one! Some bovine appetites, which find some fodder in every field. For like reasons we sometimes eat sorrel and say we love it, that we may return the hospitality of Nature by exhibiting a good appetite.

### THE RIVER'S CROP

*July* 20, 1851. The river, too, steadily yields its crop. In louring days it is remarkable how many villagers resort to it. It is of more worth than many gardens. I meet one, late in the afternoon, going to the river with his basket on his arm and his pole in hand, not ambitious to catch pickerel this time, but he thinks he may perhaps get a mess of small fish. These [*sic*] kind of values are real and important, though but little appreciated, and he is not a wise legislator who underrates them and allows the bridges to be built low so as to prevent the passage of small boats. The town is but little conscious how much interest it has in the river, and might vote it away any day thoughtlessly. There is always to be seen either some unshaven wading man, an old mower of the river meadows, familiar with water, vibrating his long pole over the lagoons of the off-shore pads, or else some solitary fisher, in a boat behind the willows, like a mote in the sunbeams reflecting the light; and who can tell how many a mess of river fish is daily cooked in the town? They are an important article of food to many a poor family.

### THE GENTLEMAN

*July* 21, 1851. Men are very generally spoiled by being so civil and well-disposed. You can have no profitable conversation with them, they are so conciliatory, determined to agree with you. They exhibit such long-suffering and kindness in a short interview. I would meet with some provoking strangeness, so that we may be guest and host and refresh one another. It is possible for a man wholly to disappear and be merged in his manners. The thousand and one gentlemen whom I meet, I meet despairingly and but to part from them, for I am not cheered by the hope of any rudeness from them. A cross man, a coarse man, an eccentric man, a silent, a man who does not drill well, — of him there is some hope. Your gentlemen, they are all alike. They utter their opinions as if it was not a man that uttered them. It is 'just as you please;' they are indifferent to everything. They will talk with you for nothing. The interesting man will rather avoid you, and it is a rare chance if you get so far as talk with him. The laborers whom I know, the loafers, fishers, and hunters, I can spin yarns with profitably, for it is hands off; they are they and I am I still; they do not come to me and quarter themselves on me for a day or an hour to be treated politely, they do not cast themselves on me for entertainment, they do not approach me with a flag of truce. They do not go out of themselves to meet me. I am never electrified by my gentleman; he is not an electric eel, but one of the common kind that slip through your hands, however hard you clutch them, and leave them covered with slime.

## SUMMER EVENING IN THE VILLAGE

*July* 21, 1851. 8.30 P.M. — The streets of the village are much more interesting to me at this hour of a summer evening than by day. Neighbors, and also farmers, come a-shopping after their day's haying, are chatting in the streets, and I hear the sound of many musical instruments and of singing from various houses. For a short hour or two the inhabitants are sensibly employed. The evening is devoted to poetry, such as the villagers can appreciate.

## A FARMER OF SENTIMENT

*July* 21, 1851. How rare to meet with a farmer who is a man of sentiment! Yet there was one, Gen. Joshua Buttrick, who died the other day, who is said to have lived in his sentiments. He used to say that the smell of burning powder excited him.

## CITY CHILDREN

*July* 25, 1851. *Friday*. Started for Clark's Island at 7 A.M.

At 9 A.M. took the Hingham boat and was landed at Hull. There was a pleasure party on board, apparently boys and girls belonging to the South End, going to Hingham. There was a large proportion of ill-dressed and ill-mannered boys of Irish extraction. A sad sight to behold! Little boys of twelve years, prematurely old, sucking cigars! I felt that if I were their mothers I should whip them and send them to bed. Such children should be dealt with as for stealing or impurity. The opening of this valve for the safety of the city! Oh, what a wretched resource! What right have parents to beget, to bring up, and attempt to *educate* children in a city? I thought of infanticide among the Orientals with complacency. I seemed to hear infant voices lisp, 'Give us a fair chance, parents.' There is no such squalidness in the

country. You would have said that they must all have come from the house of correction and the farm-school, but such a company do the boys in Boston streets make. The birds have more care for their young, — where they place their nests. What are a city's charities? She cannot be charitable any more than the old philosopher could move the earth, unless she has a resting-place without herself. A true culture is more possible to the savage than to the boy of average intellect, born of average parents, in a great city. I believe that they perish miserably. How can they be kept clean, physically or morally? It is folly to attempt to educate children within a city; the first step must be to remove them out of it. It seemed a groping and helpless philanthropy that I heard of.

I heard a boy telling the story of Nix's Mate to some girls, as we passed that spot, how 'he said, "If I am guilty, this island will remain; but if I am innocent, it will be washed away," and now it is all washed away.' This was a simple and strong expression of feeling suitable to the occasion, by which he committed the evidence of his innocence to the dumb isle, such as the boy could appreciate, a proper sailor's legend; and I was reminded that it is the illiterate and un-imaginative class that seizes on and transmits the legends in which the more cultivated delight. No fastidious poet dwelling in Boston had tampered with it, — no narrow poet, but broad mankind, sailors from all ports sailing by. They, sitting on the deck, were the literary academy that sat upon its periods.

## DANIEL WEBSTER'S FARM

*July* 27, 1851. A neighbor of Webster's told me that he had hard on to sixteen hundred acres and was still buying more, — a farm and factory within the year; cultivated a hundred and fifty acres. I saw twelve acres of potatoes together, the same of rye and wheat, and more methinks of buckwheat. Fifteen or sixteen men, Irish mostly, at ten dollars a month, doing the work of fifty, with a Yankee overseer, long a resident of Marshfield, named Wright. Would eat only the produce of his farm during the few weeks he was at home, — brown bread and butter and milk, — and sent out for a pig's cheek to eat with his greens. Ate only what grew on his farm, but drank more than ran on his farm.

## A MACKEREL SCHOONER

*July* 27, 1851. Took refuge from the rain at a Mr. Stetson's in Duxbury....

Sailed with tavern-keeper Winsor, who was going out mackereling. Seven men, stripping up their clothes, each bearing an armful of wood and one some new potatoes, walked to the boats, then shoved them out a dozen rods over the mud, then rowed half a mile to the schooner of forty-three tons. They expected to be gone about a week, and to begin to fish perhaps the next morning. Fresh mackerel which they carried to Boston. Had four dories, and commonly fished from them. Else they fished on the starboard side aft, where their lines hung ready with the old baits on, two to a man. I had the experience of going on a mackerel cruise.

They went aboard their schooner in a leisurely way this Sunday evening, with a fair but very slight wind, the sun now setting clear and shining on the vessel after several thunder-showers. I was struck by the small quantity of supplies which they appeared to take. We climbed aboard, and there we were in a mackerel schooner. The baits were not dry on the hooks. Winsor cast overboard the foul juice of mackerels mixed with rain-water which remained in his trough. There was the mill in which to grind up the mackerel for bait, and the trough to hold it, and the long-handled dipper to cast it overboard with; and already in the harbor we saw the surface rippled with schools of small mackerel. They proceeded leisurely to weigh anchor, and then to raise their two sails. There was one passenger, going for health or amusement, who had been to California. I had the experience of going a-mackereling, though I was landed on an

island before we got out of the harbor. They expected to
commence fishing the next morning. It had been a very
warm day with frequent thunder-showers. I had walked
from Cohasset to Duxbury, and had walked about the latter
town to find a passage to Clark's Island, about three miles
distant, but no boat could stir, they said, at that state of
the tide.[1] The tide was down, and boats were left high and
dry. At length I was directed to Winsor's tavern, where
perchance I might find some mackerel-fishers, who were
going to sail that night to be ready for fishing in the morning, and, as they would pass near the island, they would take
me. I found it so. Winsor himself was going. I told him he
was the very man for me; but I must wait an hour. So I
ate supper with them. Then one after another of his crew
was seen straggling to the shore, for the most part in high
boots, — some made of india-rubber, — some with their
pants stripped up. There were seven for this schooner, beside a passenger and myself. The leisurely manner in which
they proceeded struck me. I had taken off my shoes and
stockings and prepared to wade. Each of the seven took an
armful of pine wood and walked with it to the two boats,
which lay at high-water mark in the mud; then they resolved
that each should bring one more armful and that would be
enough. They had already got a barrel of water and had
some more in the schooner, also a bucket of new potatoes.
Then, dividing into two parties, we pulled and shoved the
boats a dozen rods over the mud and water till they floated,
then rowed half a mile or more over the shallow water to the
little schooner and climbed aboard. Many seals had their
heads out. We gathered about the helmsman and talked
about the compass, which was affected by the iron in the
vessel, etc., etc.

[1] Here he tells the story in a different form, showing an intention of using
it later.

## WEBSTER'S NEAREST NEIGHBOR

*July 30*, 1851. Talked with Webster's nearest neighbor, Captain Hewit, whose small farm he surrounds and endeavors in vain to buy. A fair specimen of a retired Yankee sea-captain turned farmer. Proud of the quantity of carrots he had raised on a small patch. It was better husbandry than Webster's. He told a story of his buying a cargo for his owners at St. Petersburg just as peace was declared in the last war. These men are not so remarkable for anything as the quality of hardness. The very fixedness and rigidity of their jaws and necks express a sort of adamantine hardness. This is what they have learned by contact with the elements. The man who does not grow rigid with years and experience! Where is he? What avails it to grow hard merely? The harder you are, the more brittle really, like the bones of the old. How much rarer and better to grow mellow! A sort of stone fruit the man bears commonly; a bare stone it is, without any sweet and mellow pericarp around it. It is like the peach which has dried to the stone as the season advanced; it is dwindled to a dry stone with its almond. In presence of one of these hard men I think: 'How brittle! How easily you would crack! What a poor and lame conclusion!' I can think of nothing but a stone in his head. Truly genial men do not grow [hard]. It is the result of despair, this attitude of resistance. They behave like men already driven to the wall. Notwithstanding that the speaker trembles with infirmity while he speaks, — his hand on the spade, — it is such a trembling as betrays a stony nature. His hand trembles so that the full glass of cider which he prizes to a drop will have lost half its contents before it reaches his lips, as if a tempest had arisen in it.

Hopelessly hard. But there is another view of him. He is
somebody. He has an opinion to express, if you will wait to
hear him. A certain manliness and refreshing resistance is
in him. He generally makes Webster a call, but Webster
does not want to see you more than twenty minutes. It
does not take him long to say all he has got to say. He had
not seen him to speak to him since he had come home this
time. He had sent him over a couple of fine cod the night
before. Such a man as Hewit sees not finely but coarsely.


## HAYING


*August* 17, 1851. The farmers are just finishing their
meadow-haying. (To-day is Sunday.) Those who have
early potatoes may be digging them, or doing any other job
which the haying has obliged them to postpone. For six
weeks or more this has been the farmer's work, to shave the

surface of the fields and meadows clean. This is done all
over the country. The razor is passed over these parts of
nature's face the country over. A thirteenth labor which
methinks would have broken the back of Hercules, would
have given him a memorable sweat, accomplished with what
sweating of scythes and early and late! I chance to know
one young man who has lost his life in this season's campaign,
by overdoing. In haying time some men take double wages,
and they are engaged long before in the spring. To shave
all the fields and meadows of New England clean! If men
did this but once, and not every year, we should never hear
the last of that labor; it would be more famous in each
farmer's case than Buonaparte's road over the Simplon.
It has no other bulletin but the truthful 'Farmer's Almanac.'

## EMPLOYMENTS

*August* 17, 1851. All men's employments, all trades and professions, in some of their aspects are attractive. Hence the
boy I knew, having sucked cider at a minister's cider-mill,
resolved to be a minister and make cider, not thinking, boy
as he was, how little fun there was in being a minister, willing
to purchase that pleasure at any price. When I saw the
carpenters the other day repairing Hubbard's Bridge, their
bench on the new planking they had laid over the water in
the sun and air, with no railing yet to obstruct the view, I
was almost ready to resolve that I would be a carpenter and
work on bridges, to secure a pleasant place to work. One of
the men had a fish-line cast round a sleeper, which he looked
at from time to time.

## AN IRISHMAN'S SHANTY

*August* 23, 1851. I rarely pass the shanty in the woods, where human beings are lodged, literally, no better than pigs in a sty, — little children, a grown man and his wife, and an aged grandmother living this squalid life, squatting on the ground, — but I wonder if it can be indeed true that little Julia Riordan calls this place home, comes here to rest at night and for her daily food, — in whom ladies and gentlemen in the village take an interest. Of what significance are charity and almshouses? That there they live unmolested! in one sense so many degrees below the almshouse! beneath charity! It is admirable, — Nature against almshouses. A certain wealth of nature, not poverty, it suggests. Not to identify health and contentment, aye, and independence, with the possession of this world's goods! It is not wise to waste compassion on them.

## MEN OBSERVED AS ANIMALS

*August* 23, 1851. I sometimes reproach myself because I do not find anything attractive in certain mere trivial employments of men, — that I skip men so commonly, and their affairs, — the professions and the trades, — do not elevate them at least in my thought and get some material for poetry out of them directly. I will not avoid, then, to go by where these men are repairing the stone bridge, — see if I cannot see poetry in that, if that will not yield me a reflection. It is narrow to be confined to woods and fields and

## PLATE III

*The Carpenters Repairing Hubbard's Bridge*

grand aspects of nature only. The greatest and wisest will still be related to men. Why not see men standing in the sun and casting a shadow, even as trees? May not some light be reflected from them as from the stems of trees? I will try to enjoy them as animals, at least. They are perhaps better animals than men. Do not neglect to speak of men's low life and affairs with sympathy, though you ever so speak as to suggest a contrast between them and the ideal and divine. You may be excused if you are always pathetic, but do not refuse to recognize.

## A FORMALIST

*September* 6, 1851. The other afternoon I met Sam H——walking on the railroad between the depot and the back road. It was something quite novel to see him there, though the railroad there is only a short thoroughfare to the public road. It then occurred to me that I had never met Mr. H. on the railroad, though he walks every day, and moreover that it would be quite impossible for him to walk on the railroad, such a formalist as he is, such strait-jackets we weave for ourselves. He could do nothing that was not sanctioned by the longest use of men, and as men had voted in all their assemblies from the first to travel on the public way, he would confine himself to that. It would no doubt seem to him very improper, not to say undignified, to walk on the railroad; and then, is it not forbidden by the railroad corporations? I was sure he could not keep the railroad, but was merely using the thoroughfare here which a thousand pioneers had prepared for him. I stood to see what he would do. He turned off the rails directly on to the back road and pursued his walk. A passing train will never meet him on the railroad causeway.

## THE STONE-MASON'S CRAFT

*September* 11, 1851. Every artisan learns positively something by his trade. Each craft is familiar with a few simple, well-known, well-established facts, not requiring any genius to discover, but mere use and familiarity. You may go by the man at his work in the street every day of your life, and though he is there before you, carrying into practice certain essential information, you shall never be the wiser. Each trade is in fact a craft, a cunning, a covering an ability; and its methods are the result of a long experience. There sits a stone-mason, splitting Westford granite for fence-posts. Egypt has perchance taught New England something in this matter. His hammer, his chisels, his wedges, his shims or half-rounds, his iron spoon, — I suspect that these tools are hoary with age as with granite dust. He learns as easily where the best granite comes from as he learns how to erect that screen to keep off the sun. He knows that he can drill faster into a large stone than a small one, because there is less jar and yielding. He deals in stone as the carpenter in lumber. In many of his operations only the materials are different. His work is slow and expensive. Nature is here hard to be overcome. He wears up one or two drills in splitting a single stone. He must sharpen his tools oftener than the carpenter. He fights with granite. He knows the temper of the rocks. He grows stony himself. His tread is ponderous and steady like the fall of a rock. And yet by patience and art he splits a stone as surely as the carpenter or woodcutter a log. So much time and perseverance will accomplish. One would say that mankind had much less moral than physical energy, that any day you see men following the trade of splitting rocks, who yet shrink from undertaking apparently less arduous moral labors, the solving of moral problems. See how surely he proceeds. He does not hesitate to drill a dozen holes, each one the labor of a day or two for a savage; he carefully takes out the dust with his iron spoon; he inserts his wedges, one in each hole, and protects the sides of the holes and gives resistance to his wedges by thin pieces of half-round iron (or shims); he marks the red line which he has drawn, with his chisel, carefully cutting it straight; and then how carefully he drives each wedge in succession, fearful lest he should not have a good split!

The habit of looking at men in the gross makes their lives have less of human interest for us. But though there are crowds of laborers before us, yet each one leads his little epic life each day. There is the stone-mason, who, methought, was simply a stony man that hammered stone from breakfast to dinner, and dinner to supper, and then went to his slumbers. But he, I find, is even a man like myself, for he feels the heat of the sun and has raised some boards on a frame to protect him. And now, at mid-forenoon, I see his wife and child have come and brought him drink and meat for his lunch and to assuage the stoniness of his labor, and sit to chat with him.

There are many rocks lying there for him to split from end to end, and he will surely do it. This only at the command of luxury, since stone posts are preferred to wood. But how many moral blocks are lying there in every man's yard, which he surely will not split nor earnestly endeavor to split. There lie the blocks which will surely get split, but here lie the blocks which will surely not get split. Do we say it is too hard for human faculties? But does not the mason dull a basketful of steel chisels in a day, and yet, by sharpening them again and tempering them aright, succeed? Moral effort! Difficulty to be overcome! ! ! Why, men work in stone, and sharpen their drills when they go home to dinner!

## SELECTMEN

*September* 16, 1851. Met the selectmen of Sudbury, —— and ——. I trust that towns will remember that they are supposed to be fairly represented by their *select* men. From the specimen which Acton sent, I should judge that the inhabitants of that town were made up of a mixture of quiet, respectable, and even gentlemanly farmer people, well to do in the world, with a rather boisterous, coarse, and a little self-willed class; that the inhabitants of Sudbury are farmers almost exclusively, exceedingly rough and countrified and more illiterate than usual, very tenacious of their rights and dignities and difficult to deal with; that the inhabitants of Lincoln yield sooner than usual to the influence of the rising generation, and are a mixture of rather simple but clever with a well-informed and trustworthy people; that the inhabitants of Bedford are mechanics, who aspire to keep up with the age, with some of the polish of society, mingled with substantial and rather intelligent farmers.

## THE RETIRED LIFE OF A FARMER

*September* 21, 1851. The retirement in which Green [1] has lived for nearly eighty years in Carlisle is a retirement very different from and much greater than that in which the pioneer dwells at the West; for the latter dwells within sound of the surf of those billows of migration which are breaking on the shores around him, or near him, of the West, but those billows have long since swept over the spot which Green inhabits, and left him in the calm sea. There is somewhat exceedingly pathetic to think of in such a life as he must have lived, — with no more to redeem it, — such a life as an average Carlisle man may be supposed to live drawn out to eighty years. And he has died, perchance, and there is nothing but the mark of his cider-mill left. Here was the cider-mill, and there the orchard, and there the hog-pasture; and so men lived, and ate, and drank, and passed away, — like vermin. Their long life was mere duration. As respectable is the life of the woodchucks, which perpetuate their race in the orchard still. That is the life of these *selectmen* (!) spun out. They will be forgotten in a few years, even by such as themselves, like vermin. They will be known only like Kibbe, who is said to have been a large man who weighed two hundred and fifty, who had five or six heavy daughters who rode to Concord meeting-house on horseback, taking turns, — they were so heavy that only one could ride at once. What, then, would redeem such a life? We only know that they ate, and drank, and built barns, and died and were buried, and still, perchance, their tombstones cumber the ground. But if I could know that there was ever entertained over their cellar-hole some divine

[1] Isaiah Green.

thought, which came as a messenger of the gods, that he who resided here acted once in his life from a noble impulse, rising superior to his grovelling and penurious life, if only a single verse of poetry or of poetic prose had ever been written or spoken or conceived here beyond a doubt, I should not think it in vain that man had lived here. It would to some extent be true then that God had lived here. That all his life he lived only as a farmer — as the most valuable stock only on a farm — and in no moments as a man!

### AN IRISHMAN'S ANSWER

*September* 24, 1851. Behind Miles's, Darius Miles's, that was, I asked an Irishman how many potatoes he could dig in a day, wishing to know how well they yielded. 'Well, I don't keep any account,' he answered; 'I scratch away, and let the day's work praise itself.' Aye, there's the difference between the Irishman and the Yankee; the Yankee keeps an account. The simple honesty of the Irish pleases me.

*September* 25, 1851. I was struck by the fitness of the expression chosen by the Irishman yesterday, — 'I let the day's work praise itself.' It was more pertinent than a scholar could have selected. But the Irishman does not trouble himself to inquire if the day's work has not reason to blame itself.

A BUSY FARMER

*September* 29, 1851. Found Hosmer [1] carting out manure from under his barn to make room for the winter. He said he was tired of farming, he was too old. Quoted Webster as saying that he had never eaten the bread of idleness for a single day, and thought that Lord Brougham might have said as much with truth while he was in the opposition, but he did not know that he could say as much of himself. However, he did not wish to be idle, he merely wished to rest.

[1] Edmund Hosmer, who lived at this time on the Lincoln road near Goose Pond. His daughters were among the last of the Concordians to treasure personal recollections of Thoreau.

## AIDING A FUGITIVE SLAVE

*October* 1, 1851. 5 P.M. — Just put a fugitive slave, who has taken the name of Henry Williams, into the cars for Canada. He escaped from Stafford County, Virginia, to Boston last October; has been in Shadrach's place at the Cornhill Coffee-House; had been corresponding through an agent with his master, who is his father, about buying himself, his master asking $600, but he having been able to raise only $500. Heard that there were writs out for two Williamses, fugitives, and was informed by his fellow-servants and employer that Augerhole Burns and others of the police had called for him when he was out. Accordingly fled to Concord last night on foot, bringing a letter to our family from Mr. Lovejoy of Cambridge and another which Garrison had formerly given him on another occasion. He lodged with us, and waited in the house till funds were collected with which to forward him. Intended to dispatch him at noon through to Burlington, but when I went to buy his ticket, saw one at the depot who looked and behaved so much like a Boston policeman that I did not venture that time. An intelligent and very well-behaved man, a mulatto. . . .

The slave said he could guide himself by many other stars than the north star, whose rising and setting he knew. They steered for the north star even when it had got round and appeared to them to be in the south. They frequently followed the telegraph when there was no railroad. The slaves bring many superstitions from Africa. The fugitives sometimes superstitiously carry a turf in their hats, thinking that their success depends on it.

## A POETICAL FARMER

*October* 4, 1851. Minott [1] was telling me to-day that he used to know a man in Lincoln who had no floor to his barn, but waited till the ground froze, then swept it clean in his barn and threshed his grain on it. He also used to see men threshing their buckwheat in the field where it grew, having just taken off the surface down to a hardpan.

Minott used the word 'gavel' to describe a parcel of stalks cast on the ground to dry. His are good old English words, and I am always sure to find them in the dictionary, though I never heard them before in my life.

I was admiring his corn-stalks disposed about the barn to dry, over or astride the braces and the timbers, of such a fresh, clean, and handsome green, retaining their strength and nutritive properties so, unlike the gross and careless husbandry of speculating, money-making farmers, who suffer their stalks to remain out till they are dry and dingy and black as chips.

Minott is, perhaps, the most poetical farmer — who most realizes to me the poetry of the farmer's life — that I know. He does nothing with haste and drudgery, but as if he loved it. He makes the most of his labor, and takes infinite satisfaction in every part of it. He is not looking forward to the sale of his crops or any pecuniary profit, but he is paid by the constant satisfaction which his labor yields him. He has not too much land to trouble him, — too much work to do, — no hired man nor boy, — but simply to amuse himself and live. He cares not so much to raise a large crop as to do his work well. He knows every pin and nail in his barn. If another linter is to be floored, he lets no hired man rob him

[1] George Minott, who lived on the Boston road not far from Emerson.

of that amusement, but he goes slowly to the woods and, at his leisure, selects a pitch pine tree, cuts it, and hauls it or gets it hauled to the mill; and so he knows the history of his barn floor.

Farming is an amusement which has lasted him longer than gunning or fishing. He is never in a hurry to get his garden planted and yet it is always planted soon enough, and none in the town is kept so beautifully clean.

He always prophesies a failure of the crops, and yet is satisfied with what he gets. His barn floor is fastened down with oak pins, and he prefers them to iron spikes, which he says will rust and give way. He handles and amuses himself with every ear of his corn crop as much as a child with its playthings, and so his small crop goes a great way. He might well cry if it were carried to market. The seed of weeds is no longer in his soil.

He loves to walk in a swamp in windy weather and hear the wind groan through the pines. He keeps a cat in his barn to catch the mice. He indulges in no luxury of food or dress or furniture, yet he is not penurious but merely simple. If his sister dies before him, he may have to go to the alms-house in his old age; yet he is not poor, for he does not want riches. He gets out of each manipulation in the farmers' operations a fund of entertainment which the speculating drudge hardly knows. With never-failing rheumatism and trembling hands, he seems yet to enjoy perennial health. Though he never reads a book, — since he has finished the 'Naval Monument,' — he speaks the best of English.

## FISH-SPEARERS

*October* 6, 1851.   Saw some fishermen kindling their fire for
spearing by the riverside. It was a lurid, reddish blaze,
contrasting with the white light of the moon, with dense
volumes of black smoke from the burning pitch pine roots
rolling upward in the form of an inverted pyramid. The
blaze reflected in the water, almost as distinct as the substance. It looked like tarring a ship on the shore of the Styx
or Cocytus. For it is still and dark, notwithstanding the
moon, and no sound but the crackling of the fire. The fishermen can be seen only near at hand, though their fire is visible
far away; and then they appear as dusky, fuliginous figures,
half enveloped in smoke, seen only by their enlightened
sides. Like devils they look, clad in old coats to defend themselves from the fogs, one standing up forward holding the
spear ready to dart, while the smoke and flames are blown
in his face, the other paddling the boat slowly and silently
along close to the shore with almost imperceptible motion.

## LAUDATOR TEMPORIS ACTI

*October* 12, 1851.   Minott shells all his corn by hand. He
has got a boxful ready for the mill. He will not winnow it,
for he says the chaff (?) makes it lie loose and dry faster.
He tells me that Jacob Baker, who raises as fair corn as anybody, gives all the corn of his own raising to his stock, and
buys the flat yellow corn of the South for bread; and yet
the Northern corn is worth the most per bushel. Minott did

not like this kind of farming any better than I. Baker also buys a great quantity of 'shorts' below for his cows, to make more milk. He remembers when a Prescott, who lived where E. Hosmer does, used to let his hogs run in the woods in the fall, and they grew quite fat on the acorns, etc., they found, but now there are few nuts, and it is against the law. He tells me of places in the woods which to his eyes are unchanged since he was a boy, as natural as life. He tells me, then, that in some respects he is still a boy. And yet the gray squirrels were ten then to one now. But for the most part, he says, the world is turned upside down.

### MINOTT'S SQUIRREL-HUNTING

*October* 12, 1851. Minott calls the stake-driver 'belchersquelcher.' Says he has seen them when making the noise. They go *slug-toot*, *slug-toot*, *slug-toot*. Told me of his hunting gray squirrels with old Colonel Brooks's hound. How the latter came into the yard one day, and he spoke to him, patted him, went into the house, took down his gun marked London, thought he would go a-squirrel-hunting. Went over among the ledges, away from Brooks's, for Tige had a dreadful strong voice and could be heard as far as a cannon, and he was plaguy afraid Brooks would hear him. How Tige treed them on the oaks on the plain below the Cliffs. He could tell by his bark when he had treed one; he never told a lie. And so he got six or seven. How Tige told him from a distance that he had got one, but when he came up he could see nothing; but still he knew that Tige never told a lie, and at length he saw his head, in a crotch high up in the top of a very tall oak, and though he didn't expect to get him, he knocked him over.

## MISS MARY EMERSON

*November* 13, 1851.  Just spent a couple of hours (eight to ten) with Miss Mary Emerson [1] at Holbrook's.  The wittiest and most vivacious woman that I know, certainly that woman among my acquaintance whom it is most profitable to meet, the least frivolous, who will most surely provoke to good conversation and the expression of what is in you. She is singular, among women at least, in being really and perseveringly interested to know what thinkers think.  She relates herself surely to the intellectual where she goes.  It is perhaps her greatest praise and peculiarity that she, more surely than any other woman, gives her companion occasion to utter his best thought.  In spite of her own biases, she can entertain a large thought with hospitality, and is not prevented by any intellectuality in it, as women commonly are. In short, she is a genius, as woman seldom is, reminding you less often of her sex than any woman whom I know.  In that sense she is capable of a masculine appreciation of poetry and philosophy.  I never talked with any other woman who I thought accompanied me so far in describing a poetic experience.  Miss Fuller is the only woman I think of in this connection, and of her rather from her fame than from any knowledge of her.  Miss Emerson expressed to-night a singular want of respect for her own sex, saying that they were frivolous almost without exception, that woman was the weaker vessel, etc.; that into whatever family she might go, she depended more upon the 'clown' for society than upon the lady of the house.  Men are more likely to have opinions of their own.

   [1] Mary Moody Emerson (1774–1863), aunt of Ralph Waldo Emerson, over whose development she exercised a strong influence.

### AN EVENING PARTY

*November* 14, 1851. In the evening went to a party. It is
a bad place to go to, — thirty or forty persons, mostly
young women, in a small room, warm and noisy. Was introduced to two young women. The first one was as lively
and loquacious as a chickadee; had been accustomed to the
society of watering-places, and therefore could get no re-
freshment out of such a dry fellow as I. The other was said
to be pretty-looking, but I rarely look people in their faces,
and, moreover, I could not hear what she said, there was
such a clacking, — could only see the motion of her lips
when I looked that way. I could imagine better places for
conversation, where there should be a certain degree of
silence surrounding you, and less than forty talking at once.
Why, this afternoon, even, I did better. There was old Mr.
Joseph Hosmer and I ate our luncheon of cracker and cheese
together in the woods. I heard all he said, though it was
not much, to be sure, and he could hear me. And then he
talked out of such a glorious repose, taking a leisurely bite
at the cracker and cheese between his words; and so some of
him was communicated to me, and some of me to him, I
trust.

### IDEAS

*November* 15, 1851. Asked Therien ¹ this afternoon if he
had got a new idea this summer. 'Good Lord!' says he, 'a

¹ Aleck Therien, the French-Canadian woodchopper who figures anonymously
in *Walden*.

# PLATE IV

*Thoreau and Miss Mary Emerson*

man that has to work as I do, if he does not forget the ideas he has had, he will do well. Maybe the man you work with is inclined to race; then, by gorry, your mind must be there; you think of weeds.'

## THE SABBATH

*November* 16, 1851. A man lately preached here against the abuse of the Sabbath and recommended to walk in the fields and dance on that day, — good advice enough, which may take effect after a while. But with the mass of men the reason is convinced long before the life is. They may see the Church and the Sabbath to be false, but nothing else to be true. One woman in the neighborhood says, 'Nobody can hear Mr. —— preach, — hear him through, — without seeing that he is a good man.' 'Well, is there any truth in what he says?' asks another. 'Oh, yes, it's true enough, but then it won't do; you know it won't do. Now there's our George, he's got the whole of it; and when I say, "Come, George, put on your things and go along to meeting," he says, "No, Mother, I'm going out into the fields." It won't do.' The fact is, this woman has not character and religion enough to exert a controlling influence over her children by her example, and knows of no such police as the Church and the minister.

## 'PERCH' HOSMER

*November* 18, 1851. Deacon Brown told me to-day of a tall, raw-boned fellow by the name of Hosmer who used to help draw the seine behind the Jones house, who once, when he had hauled it without getting a single shad, held up a little perch in sport above his face, to show what he had got. At that moment the perch wiggled and dropped right down his throat head foremost, and nearly suffocated him; and it was only after considerable time, during which the man suffered much, that he was extracted or forced down. He was in a worse predicament than a fish hawk would have been.[1]

## OLD MR. JOSEPH HOSMER

*November* 19, 1851. Old Mr. Joseph Hosmer, who helped me to-day, said that he used to know all about the lots, but since they've chopped off so much, and the woods have grown up, he finds himself lost. Thirty or forty years ago, when he went to meeting, he knew every face in the meeting-house, even the boys and girls, they looked so much like their parents; but after ten or twelve years they would have outgrown his knowledge entirely (they would have altered so), but he knew the old folks still, because they held their own and didn't alter. Just so he could tell the boundaries of the old wood which hadn't been cut down,

[1] We are told elsewhere that after this incident the man was known as 'Perch' Hosmer.

but the young wood altered so much in a few years that
he couldn't tell anything about it. When I asked him
why the old road which went by this swamp was so round-
about, he said he would answer me as Mr. —— —— did
him in a similar case once, — 'Why, if they had made it
straight, they wouldn't have left any room for improvement.'

## A BLUNDERING IRISHMAN

*December* 12, 1851. The Irishman (MacCarty) who helped
me survey day before yesterday would not sit on a rock
with me to eat his dinner (there being snow on the ground),
from a notion that there was nothing so deadly as sitting
on a rock, — sure to give you a cold in the back. He would
rather stand. So the doctors said, down in the Province of
New Brunswick. But I warranted him that he would not
get a cold in his back, which was half as broad again as mine,
and so he minded me as a new doctor. A gray-headed
boy, good for nothing but to eat his dinner. These Irishmen have no heads. Let me inquire strictly into a man's
descent, and if his remotest ancestors were Erse, let me
not have him to help me survey. One or two I have seen,
handy men, but I learned that their fathers, who came
from Ireland, were of the Scotch-Irish. This fellow was
sure to do the wrong thing from the best motives, and the
only time he was spry was when he was running to correct his own blunders out of his own head — and make
them worse than before, but I could not stop him; then I
saw the broad red soles of his new cowhide boots alternately rising and falling like the buckets of a dasher or

water-wheel. When he had lost his plumb and went to get it, then he showed the red soles of his boots.

### THE REAL FORM OF A MAN

*December* 13, 1851. Saw Perez Blood in his frock, — a stuttering, sure, unpretending man, who does not speak without thinking, does not guess. When I reflected how different he was from his neighbors, Conant, Mason, Hodgman, I saw that it was not so much outwardly, but that I saw an inner form. We do, indeed, see through and through each other, through the veil of the body, and see the real form and character in spite of the garment. Any coarseness or tenderness is seen and felt under whatever garb. How nakedly men appear to us! for the spiritual assists the natural eye.

### AN OLD IRISHWOMAN

*December* 31, 1851. I observed this afternoon the old Irishwoman at the shanty in the woods, sitting out on the hillside, bareheaded, in the rain and on the icy though thawing ground, knitting. She comes out, like the ground squirrel, at the least intimation of warmer weather. She will not have to go far to be buried, so close she lives to the earth, while I walk still in a greatcoat and under an umbrella. Such Irish as these are naturalizing themselves at a rapid rate, and threaten at last to displace the Yankees, as the latter have the Indians. The process of acclimation is

rapid with them; they draw long breaths in the American sick-room. What must be the philosophy of life to that woman, ready to flow down the slope with the running sand! Ah, what would I not give for her point of view! She does not use any *th*'s in her style. Yet I fear that even she may have learned to lie.

## A WOMAN LECTURER

*December* 31, 1851. This night I heard Mrs. S ——[1] lecture on womanhood. The most important fact about the lecture was that a woman said it, and in that respect it was sug-

[1] Elizabeth Oakes Smith.

gestive. Went to see her afterward, but the interview added nothing to the previous impression, rather subtracted. She was a woman in the too common sense after all. You had to fire small charges: I did not have a finger in once, for fear of blowing away all her works and so ending the game. You had to substitute courtesy for sense and argument. It requires nothing less than a chivalric feeling to sustain a conversation with a lady. I carried her lecture for her in my pocket wrapped in her handkerchief; my pocket exhales cologne to this moment. The championess of woman's rights still asks you to be a ladies' man. I can't fire a salute, even, for fear some of the guns may be shotted. I had to unshot all the guns in truth's battery and fire powder and wadding only. Certainly the heart is only for rare occasions; the intellect affords the most unfailing entertainment. It would only do to let her feel the wind of the ball. I fear that to the last woman's lectures will demand mainly courtesy from man.

### GOD WITH A LITTLE *g*

*January* 8, 1852. Reading from my manuscripts to Miss Emerson this evening and using the word 'god,' in one instance, in perchance a merely heathenish sense, she inquired hastily in a tone of dignified anxiety, 'Is that god spelt with a little *g*?' Fortunately it was. (I had brought in the word 'god' without any solemnity of voice or connection.) So I went on as if nothing had happened.

### BILL WHEELER'S LIFE AND DEATH

*January* 16, 1852. Bill Wheeler had two clumps for feet and progressed slowly, by short steps, having frozen his feet once, as I understood. Him I have been sure to meet once in five years, progressing into the town on his stubs, holding the middle of the road as if he drove an invisible herd before him, especially on a military day, — out of what confines, whose hired man having been, I never knew, — in what remote barn having quartered all these years. He seemed to belong to a different caste from other men, and reminded me of both the Indian Pariah and martyr. I understood that somebody was found to give him his drink for the few chores he could do. His meat was never referred to, he had so sublimed his life. One day since this, not long ago, I saw in my walk a kind of shelter such as woodmen might use, in the woods by the Great Meadows, made of meadow-hay cast over a rude frame. Thrusting my head in at a hole, as I am wont to do in such cases, I found Bill Wheeler there curled up asleep on the hay, who, being suddenly wakened from a sound sleep, rubbed his eyes and inquired if I found any game, thinking I was sporting. I came away reflecting much on that man's life, — how he communicated with none; how now, perchance, he did chores for none; how low he lived, perhaps from a deep principle, that he might be some mighty philosopher, greater than Socrates or Diogenes, simplifying life, returning to nature, having turned his back on towns; how many things he had put off, — luxuries, comforts, human society, even his feet, — wrestling with his thoughts. I felt even as Diogenes when he saw the boy drinking out of his hands, and threw away his cup. Here was one who went alone, did no work, and had no relatives that I knew of, was not ambitious that I could see, did not depend on the good opinion of men. Must he not see things with an impartial eye, disinterested, as a toad observes the gardener? Perchance here is one of a sect of philosophers, the only one, so simple, so abstracted in thought and life from his contemporaries, that his wisdom is indeed foolishness to them. Who knows but in his solitary meadow-hay bunk he indulges, in thought, only in triumphant satires on men? Who knows but here is a superiority to literature and such things, unexpressed and inexpressible? Who has resolved to humble and mortify himself as never man was humbled and mortified. Whose very vividness of perception, clear knowledge, and insight have made him dumb, leaving no common consciousness and ground of parlance with his kind, — or, rather, his unlike kindred! Whose news plainly is not my news nor yours. I was not sure for a moment but here was a philosopher who had left far behind him the philosophers of Greece and India, and I envied him his advantageous point of view. I was not to be deceived by a few stupid words, of course, and apparent besottedness. It was his position and career that I contemplated.

Channing[1] has great respect for McKean, he stands on so low a level. Says he's great for conversation. He never says anything, hardly answers a question, but keeps at work; never exaggerates, nor uses an exclamation, and does as he agrees to. He appears to have got his shoulder to the wheel of the universe. But the other day he went greater lengths with me, as he and Barry were sawing down a pine, both kneeling of necessity. I said it was wet work for the knees in the snow. He observed, looking up at me, 'We pray without ceasing.'

[1] William Ellery Channing (1818–1901), poet, nephew of Rev. William Ellery Channing. He lived on Main Street in the village of Concord and was Thoreau's most frequent companion on his walks.

But to return to Bill. I would have liked to know what view he took of life. A month or two after this, as I heard, he was found dead among the brush over back of the hill, — so far decomposed that his coffin was carried to his body and it was put into it with pitchforks. I have my misgivings still that he may have died a Brahmin's death, dwelling at the roots of trees at last, and been absorbed into the spirit of Brahm; though I have since been assured that he suffered from disappointed love, — was what is called love-cracked, — than which can there be any nobler suffering, any fairer death, for a human creature? — that that made him to drink, froze his feet, and did all the rest for him. Why have not the world the benefit of his long trial?

### VISITORS TO THE WALDEN HUT

*January* 17, 1852. One day two young women — a Sunday — stopped at the door of my hut and asked for some water. I answered that I had no cold water but I would lend them a dipper. They never returned the dipper, and I had a right to suppose that they came to steal. They were a disgrace to their sex and to humanity. Pariahs of the moral world. Evil spirits that thirsted not for water but threw the dipper into the lake. Such as Dante saw. What the lake to them but liquid fire and brimstone? They will never know peace till they have returned the dipper. In all the worlds this is decreed. . . .

One day an inoffensive, simple-minded pauper from the almshouse, who, with others, I often saw used as fencing-stuff, standing or sitting on a bushel in the fields to keep cattle from straying, visited me, and expressed a wish to live as I did. He told me in the simplest manner (and there-fore quite superior to anything that is called humility — it was too simple and truthful for that) that he was 'de-ficient in intellect.' These were his words. The Lord had made him so, and yet he supposed that the Lord cared for him as much as for another. Said he: 'I have always been so from my childhood; I never had much mind. It was the Lord's will, I suppose. I am weak in the head. I was not like other children.' I have rarely been so fortunate as to meet a fellow-man on such promising ground. It was so solemnly true all that he said.

### SHAMING THE IMPUDENT

*January* 17, 1852. The other day, the 14th, as I was pass-ing the further Garfield house beyond Holden's, with my pantaloons, as usual, tucked into my boots (there was no path beyond Holden's), I heard some persons in Garfield's shed, but did not look round, and when I had got a rod or two beyond, I heard some one call out impudently from the shed, quite loud, something like 'Holloa, mister! what do you think of the walking?' I turned round directly, and saw three men standing in the shed. I was resolved to dis-comfit them, — that they should prove their manhood, if they had any, and find something to say, though they had nothing before, that they should make amends to the uni-verse by feeling cheap. They should either say to my face and eye what they had said to my back, or they should feel the meanness of having to change their tone. So I called out, looking at one, 'Do you wish to speak to me, sir?' No answer. So I stepped a little nearer and repeated

the question, when one replied, 'Yes, sir.' So I advanced
with alacrity up the path they had shovelled. In the
meanwhile one ran into the house. I thought I had seen
the nearest one before. He called me by name, faintly and
with hesitation, and held out his hand half unconsciously,
which I did not decline, and I inquired gravely if he wished
to say anything to me. He could only wave me to the other
and mutter, 'My brother.' I approached *him* and repeated
the question. He looked as if he were shrinking into a
nutshell; a pitiable object he was. He looked away from me
while he began to frame some business, some surveying,
that he might wish to have done. I saw that he was drunk,
that his brother was ashamed of him, and I turned my
back on him in the outset of this indirect but drunken
apology.

### THE LITTLETON GIANT

*January* 17, 1852. Saw a teamster coming up the Boston
road this afternoon, sitting on his load, which was bags of
corn or salt, apparently, behind two horses and beating
his hands for warmth. He finally got off and walked behind, to make his blood circulate faster, and I saw that he
was a large man. But when I came near him, I found that
he was a monstrous man and dwarfed all whom he stood
by, so that I did not know whether he was large or they
were small. Yet, though he stood so high, he stooped considerably, more than anybody I think of, and he wore a
flat glazed cap to conceal his height, and when he got into
the village he sat down on his bags again. I heard him
remark to a boy that it was a cold day, and it was; but I

wondered that he should feel the cold so sensibly, for I thought it must take a long time to cool so large a body.

I learned that it was Kimball of Littleton, that probably he was not twenty. The family was not *large*. Wild, who took the census, said so, and that his sister said he couldn't do much, — health and strength not much. It troubled him that he was so large, for people looked at him. There is at once something monstrous, in the bad sense, suggested by the sight of such a man. Great size is inhuman. It is as if a man should be born with the earth attached to him. I saw him standing up on a sled, talking with the driver, while his own team went on ahead; and I supposed from their comparative height that his companion was sitting, but he proved to be standing. Such a man is so much less human; that is what may make him sad.

## MISS MARY EMERSON

*January* 18, 1852. E. Hosmer tells me that his daughter, walking with Miss Mary Emerson to some meeting or lecture, — perhaps it was Mrs. Smith's, — the latter was saying that she did not want to go, she did not think it was worth while to be running after such amusements, etc., etc. Whereupon Miss Hosmer asked, 'What do you go for, then?' 'None of your business,' was the character- istic reply. Sometimes, when a woman was speaking where gentlemen were present, she put her hand on her and said, 'Be still. I want to hear the men talk.'

## HIGGINSON AS A LECTURER

*January* 21, 1852. Heard Higginson [1] lecture to-night on Mohammed. Why did I not like it better? Can I deny that it was good? Perhaps I am bound to account to *myself* at least for any lurking dislike for what others admire and I am not *prepared* to find fault with. Well, I did not like it, then, because it did not make me like it, it did not carry me away captive. He is not simple enough. For the most part the manner overbore, choked off, and stifled, put out of sight and hearing, the matter. I was inclined to forget that he was speaking, conveying ideas; thought there had been an intermission. Never endeavor consciously to supply the tone which you think proper for certain sentences. It is as if a man whose mind was at ease should supply the tones and gestures for a man in distress who found only the words; as when one makes a speech and another behind him makes gestures. Then he reminded me of Emerson, and I could not afford to be reminded of Christ himself. Yet who can deny that it was good? But it was that intelligence, that way of viewing things (combined with much peculiar *talent*), which is the common property of this generation. A man does best when he is most himself.

[1] Thomas Wentworth Higginson.

### DANIEL FOSTER

*January* 25, 1852.  When Sophia [1] told R. Rice that Dr. B. said that Foster [2] was an infidel and was injuring the young men, etc., ' Did he?' he observed. 'Well, he is a great man. He swims in pretty deep water, but it isn't very extensive.' When she added, 'Mr. Frost says that Garrison had to apologize for printing Foster's sermon,' he said, 'Did he? Well, they may set as many back fires as they please; they won't be of any use; they'll soon go out.' She said the selectmen were going to ask seven dollars instead of five for the hall. But he said that he would build them a hall, if they would engage to give him five dollars steadily. To be sure, it would not be quite so handsome as the present, but it should have the same kind of seats.

### FOSTER'S SUCCESS

*January* 26, 1852.  Foster's success is in reaching such men as Houghton, Goodwin, Rice, McKean, Pratt, E. Hubbard, S. Barrett, and others, — Wilson, and even Dillingham; some of whom are men of sterling worth and probity, the salt of the earth, and confessedly the very best of our citizens, though the Church may have called them infidels. They were only more faithful than the rest. They did not go off at half-cock. I do not know more honest or trustworthy men than Rice, Pratt, Barrett, McKean, etc. Frost and Anger [?] might preach forever; they would never reach

[1] Thoreau's younger sister.          [2] Rev. Daniel Foster, of Concord.

these men. Houghton never realized before that the design
of any preacher was to do good to men. In this movement
of the waters, the sectarians and formalists are left floating
on chips and slivers of doctrine. In preaching to the men
whom I have named they make the mistake of preaching or
writing on the letter and not the meaning of the letter, the
creed and not the life. When a truer man comes, the assem-
bly see the difference at last between his life and the life of
his predecessors, and the doctrines of the latter properly
pass for *wind*. They say of the former, 'He hits the nail on
the head.' Every shade and degree of hypocrisy will affect
the tone of the voice, and the audience will laugh. The rum-
seller likes Foster better than Manning, though he is strenu-
ously opposed to his traffic, because he is frank and manly
with him and not all things to all men. Those men I have
named represent the healthy mind of the generation, who
have ears to hear. The man may be proud who satisfies
them.

### LITTLE JOHNNY RIORDAN [1]

They showed me little Johnny Riordan the other day, as
bright a boy of five years as ever trod our paths, whom you
could not see for five minutes without loving and honoring
him. He *lives* in what they call the *shanty* in the woods. He
had on, in the middle of January of the coldest winter we
have had for twenty years, one thickness only of ragged
cloth sewed on to his pantaloons over his little shirt, and
shoes with large holes in the toes, into which the snow got,

[1] This sketch was written on loose sheets of manuscript inclosed between the
leaves of one of Thoreau's journals. It was made up, with some revision, from
journal-entries for November 28, 1850; December 22, 1851; and January 28,
1852.

as he was obliged to confess, he who had trodden five winters under his feet! Thus clad he walked a mile to school
every day, over the bleakest of railroad causeways, where I
know by experience the grown man would frequently freeze
his ears or nose if they were not well protected, — for his
parents have no thermometer, — all to get learning and
warmth and there sit at the head of his bench. These clothes
with countless patches, which had for vehicle — O shame!
shame! — pantaloons that had been mine, they whispered
to me, set as if his mother had fitted them to a tea-kettle first.

I glimpsed him the other morning taking his last step
from his last snow-drift on to the schoolhouse door-step,
floundering still; saw not his face nor his profile, only his
mien, but saw clearly in imagination his 'old-worthy' face
behind the sober visor of his cap, and he revived to my mind
the grave nobility and magnanimity of ancient heroes. He
never was drawn in a willow wagon, but progresses by his

own brave steps. Has not the world waited for such a generation? Here he condescends to his a-b-c without one smile,
who has the lore of worlds uncounted in his brain. He speaks
not of the adventures of the causeway. What was the brav-
ery of Leonidas and his three hundred boys at the pass of
Thermopylæ to this infant's? They dared but to die; he
dares to live, and takes his reward of merit, perchance,
without relaxing his face into a smile, that does not reward
a thousandth part of his merits, that overlooks his unseen
and unrewardable merits, — Little Johnny Riordan, who
faces cold and routs it like a Persian army, who, yet innocent, carries in his knees the strength of a thousand Indras.
Not to be so tenderly nurtured as you and I forsooth? All
day he plays with his coevals and equals, and then they go to
their several homes.

I am the little Irish boy,
    That lives in the shanty.
I am five years old to-day,
    And shall soon be one and twenty.

At recess I play
With little Billy Gray,
And when school is done,
Then away I run.

And if I meet the cars,
    I get on the other track,
And then I know, whatever comes,
    I needn't look back.

Having carried off the palm in the intellectual contest
with the children of luxury, how bravely he contemplates
his destiny: —

I shall grow up
    And be a great man,
And shovel all day
    As hard as I can.

This tender gobbet for the fates, cast into a cold world, with a torn lichen leaf wrapped about him! I would rather hear that America's first-born were all slain than that his little fingers and toes should feel cold while I am warm. Is man so cheap that he cannot be clothed but with a mat or a rag? that we should abandon to him our *wornout* clothes or our *cold* victuals? Infancy pleads with equal eloquence from all platforms. Rather let the mature rich wear the rags and insufficient clothing, the infant poor and rich, if any, wear the costly furs, the purple and fine linen. Our charitable institutions are an insult to humanity, — a charity which dispenses the crumbs that fall from its overloaded tables! whose waste and whose example helped to produce that poverty!

While the charitable waddle about cased in furs and finery, this boy, lively as a cricket, passes them on his way to school. I see that, for the present, the child is happy, is not puny, and has all the wonders of nature for his toys. Have I not faith that his tenderness will in some way be cherished and protected, as the buds of spring in the remotest wintry dell no less than in the garden and summer-house?

### CHANNING AS A LECTURER

*January* 29, 1852. Heard C.[1] lecture to-night. It was a bushel of nuts. Perhaps the most original lecture I ever heard. Ever so unexpected, not to be foretold, and so sententious that you could not look at him and take his thought at the same time. You had to give your undivided attention to the thoughts, for you were not assisted by set phrases

[1] William Ellery Channing, the younger.

or modes of speech intervening. There was no sloping up or down to or from his points. It was all genius, no talent. It required more close attention, more abstraction from surrounding circumstances, than any lecture I have heard. For, well as I know C., he more than any man disappoints my expectation. When I see him in the desk, hear him, I cannot realize that I ever saw him before. He will be strange, unexpected, to his best acquaintance. I cannot associate the lecturer with the companion of my walks. It was from so original and peculiar a point of view, yet just to himself in the main, that I doubt if three in the audience apprehended a tithe that he said. It was so hard to hear that doubtless few made the exertion. A thick succession of mountain passes and no intermediate slopes and plains. Other lectures, even the best, in which so much space is given to the elaborate development of a few ideas, seemed somewhat meagre in comparison. Yet it would be how much more glorious if talent were added to genius, if there were a just arrangement and development of the thoughts, and each step were not a leap, but he ran a space to take a yet higher leap!

Most of the spectators sat in front of the performer, but here was one who, by accident, sat all the while on one side, and his report was peculiar and startling.

### MANNERS

*January* 31, 1852. —— is too grand for me. He belongs to the nobility and wears their cloak and manners; is attracted to Plato, not to Socrates, I fear partly because the latter's life and associates were too humble. I am a commoner. To me there is something devilish in manners. The best manners is nakedness of manners. I should value E.'s praise more, which is always so discriminating, if there were not some alloy of patronage and hence of flattery about it. In that respect he is like ——;[1] they flatter you, but themselves more. Praise should be spoken as simply and naturally as a flower emits its fragrance.

## THE IRISH

*February* 8, 1852. Carried a new cloak to Johnny Riordan. I found that the shanty was warmed by the simple social relations of the Irish. On Sunday they come from the town and stand in the doorway and so keep out the cold. One is not cold among his brothers and sisters. What if there is less fire on the hearth, if there is more in the heart!

These Irish are not succeeding so ill after all. The little boy goes to the primary school and proves a forward boy there, and the mother's brother, who has let himself in the village, tells me that he takes the 'Flag of our Union' (if that is the paper edited by an Irishman). It is musical news to hear that Johnny does not love to be kept at home from school in deep snows.

[1] In the manuscript journal the first dash (made in pencil) stood for a single initial carefully scratched out; the second, for a full name, also erased.

### THE FISHERMAN

*February* 9, 1852.  Met Sudbury Haines on the river before
the Cliffs, come a-fishing.  Wearing an old coat, much
patched, with many colors.  He represents the Indian still.
The very patches in his coat and his improvident life do so.
I feel that he is as essential a part, nevertheless, of our community as the lawyer in the village.  He tells me that he
caught three pickerel here the other day that weighed seven
pounds all together.  It is the old story.  The fisherman is a
natural story-teller.  No man's imagination plays more
pranks than his, while he is tending his reels and trotting
from one to another, or watching his cork in summer.  He
is ever waiting for the sky to fall.  He has sent out a venture.  He has a ticket in the lottery of fate, and who knows
what it may draw?  He ever expects to catch a bigger fish
yet.  He is the most patient and believing of men.  Who else
will stand so long in wet places?  When the haymaker runs
to shelter, he takes down his pole and bends his steps to the
river, glad to have a leisure day.  He is more like an inhabitant of nature.  The weather concerns him.  He is an observer
of her phenomena.

### MR. JOE HOSMER ON OAK WOOD

*March* 6, 1852.  Old Mr. Joe Hosmer chopping wood at his
door.  He is full of meat.  Had a crack with him.  I told him
I was studying lichens, pointing to his wood.  He thought I
meant the wood itself.  Well, he supposed he'd had more to

do with wood than I had. 'Now,' said he, 'there are two
kinds of white oak. Most people wouldn't notice it. When
I've been chopping, say along in March, after the sap begins
to start, I'll sometimes come to an oak that will color my
axe steel-blue like a sword-blade. Well, that oak is fine-
grained and heavier than the common, and I call it blue
white oak, for no other blues my axe so. Then there are
two kinds of black oak, or yellow-bark. One is the mean
black oak, or bastard. Then there's a kind of red oak smells
like urine three or four days old.' It was really respectable
in him that he avoided using the vulgar name of this oak.
In an old man like him it was a true delicacy.

### A HOT AFTERNOON

*June* 15, 1852. The farmhouses under their shady trees
(Baker's) look as if the inhabitants were taking their siesta
at this hour. . . . Why does work go forward now? No scour-
ing of tubs or cans now. The cat and all are gone to sleep,
preparing for an early tea, excepting the indefatigable,
never-resting hoers in the corn-field, who have carried a jug
of molasses and water to the field and will wring their shirts
to-night. I shall ere long hear the horn blow for their early
tea. The wife or the hired Irishwoman steps to the door and
blows the long tin horn, a cheering sound to the laborers in
the field.

## EDMUND HOSMER

*July* 6, 1852. Hosmer is haying, but inclined to talk as usual. I blowed on his horn at supper-time. I asked if I should do any harm if I sounded it. He said no, but I called Mrs. Hosmer back, who was on her way to the village, though I blowed it but poorly. I was surprised to find how much skill and breath it took, depending on the size of the throat. Let blow a horn, says Robin, that good fellowship may us know. Where could a man go to practice on the horn, unless he went round to the farmer's at mealtime?

I am disappointed that Hosmer, the most intelligent farmer in Concord, and perchance in Middlesex, who admits that he has property enough for his use without accumulating more, and talks of leaving off hard work, letting his farm, and spending the rest of his days easier and better, cannot yet think of any method of employing himself but in work with his hands; only he would have a little less of it. Much as he is inclined to speculation in conversation — giving up any work to it for the time — and long-headed as he is, he talks of working for a neighbor for a day now and then and taking his dollar. He 'would not like to spend his time sitting on the mill-dam.' He has not even planned an essentially better life.

## BATHING

*July* 8, 1852. I am inclined to think bathing almost one of the necessaries of life, but it is surprising how indifferent some are to it. What a coarse, foul, busy life we lead, compared even with the South-Sea-Islanders, in some respects. Truant boys steal away to bathe, but the farmers, who most need it, rarely dip their bodies into the streams or ponds. M—— was telling me last night that he had thought of bathing when he had done his hoeing, — of taking some soap and going down to Walden and giving himself a good scrubbing, — but something had occurred to prevent it, and now he will go unwashed to the harvesting, aye, even till the next hoeing is over. Better the faith and practice of the Hindoos who worship the sacred Ganges. We have not faith enough in the Musketaquid to wash in it, even after hoeing. Men stay on shore, keep themselves dry, and drink rum. Pray what were rivers made for? One farmer, who came to bathe in Walden one Sunday while I lived there, told me it was the first bath he had had for fifteen years. Now what kind of religion could his be? Or was it any better than a Hindoo's?

## HONEST TOIL

*July* 24, 1852. Just after sunrise this morning I noticed Hayden walking beside his team, which was slowly drawing a heavy hewn stone swung under the axle, surrounded by an atmosphere of industry, his day's work begun. Honest, peaceful industry, conserving the world, which all men respect, which society had consecrated. A reproach to all sluggards and idlers. Pausing abreast the shoulders of his oxen and half turning round, with a flourish of his merciful whip, while they gained their length on him. And I thought, such is the labor which the American Congress exists to protect, — honest, manly toil. His brow has commenced to sweat. Honest as the day is long. One of the sacred band doing the needful but irksome drudgery. Toil that makes his bread taste sweet, and keeps society sweet. The day went by, and at evening I passed a rich man's yard, who keeps many servants and foolishly spends much money while he adds nothing to the common stock, and there I saw Hayden's stone lying beside a whimsical structure intended to adorn this Lord Timothy Dexter's mansion, and the dignity forthwith departed from Hayden's labor, in my eyes.

## A. BRONSON ALCOTT

*August* 11, 1852. Alcott here the 9th and 10th. He, the spiritual philosopher, is, and has been for some months, devoted to the study of his own genealogy, — he whom only the genealogy of humanity, the descent of man from God, should concern! He has been to his native town of Wolcott, Connecticut, on this errand, has faithfully perused the records of some fifteen towns, has read the epitaphs in as many churchyards, and, wherever he found the name Alcock, excerpted it and all connected with it, — for he is delighted to discover that the original name was All-*cock* and meant something, that some grandfather or great-grandfather bore it, Philip Alcock (though his son wisely enough changed it to Alcott). He who wrote of Human Culture, he who conducted the Conversations on the Gospels, he who discoursed of Sleep, Health, Worship, Friendship, etc., last winter, now reading the wills and the epitaphs of the Alcocks with the zeal of a professed antiquarian and genealogist! He has discovered that one George Alcock (afterwards Deacon George) came over with Winthrop in 1630 and settled in Roxbury. Has read Eliot's account of him in the Church records and been caught by a passage in which his character is de-

scribed by Eliot as being of 'good savor.' I think it is. But
he has by no means made out his descent from him. Only
knows that that family owned lands in Woodstock, Connecticut. Nevertheless the similarity of name is enough, and
he pursues the least trace of it. Has visited a crockery-
dealer in Boston who trades with Alcocks of Staffordshire
(?), England, *great* potters who took a prize at the world's
fair. Has through him obtained a cup or so with the name
of the maker Alcock on it. Has it at his house. Has got the
dealer to describe the persons of those Staffordshire Alcocks,
and finds them to be of the right type, even to their noses.
He knew they must be so. Has visited the tomb of Dr. John
Alcock in the Granary Burying Ground, read, and copied it.
Has visited also the only bearer of the name in Boston, a
sail-maker perchance, — though there is no evidence of the
slightest connection except through Adam, — and communicated with him. He says I should survey Concord and
put down every house exactly as it stands with the name.
Admires the manuscript of the old records; more pleasing
than print. Has some design to collect and print epitaphs.
Thinks they should be collected and printed *verbatim et
literatim*, every one in every yard, with a perfect index
added, so that persons engaged in such pursuits as himself
might be absolutely sure, when they turned to the name
Alcock, for instance, to find it if it was there, and not have
to look over the whole yard. Talks of going to England —
says it would be in his way — to visit the Alcocks of Staffordshire. Has gone now to find where lie the three thousand
acres granted to the Roxbury family in 16— 'on the Assa-
bett,' and has talked with a lawyer about the possibility of
breaking the title, etc., etc., from time to time pulling out
a long notebook from his bosom, with epitaphs and the like
copied into it. Had copied into it the epitaph of my grand-
mother-in-law which he came across in some graveyard (in
Charlestown?), thinking 'it would interest me!'

## PLATE V

*Mr. Alcott in the Granary Burying Ground in Boston*

**CHANNING AND HIS DOG**

*August* 11, 1852.   C. says he keeps a dog for society, to stir up the air of the room when it becomes dead, for he experiences awful solitudes. Another time thinks we must cultivate the social qualities, perhaps had better keep two dogs apiece.

**BEE-HUNTING**

*September* 30, 1852.   To Fair Haven Pond, bee-hunting, — Pratt, Rice, Hastings, and myself, in a wagon.

A fine, clear day after the coolest night and severest frost we have had. The apparatus was, first a simple round tin box about four and a half inches in diameter and one and a half inches deep, containing a piece of empty honeycomb of its own size and form, filling it within a third of an inch of the top; also another, *wooden* box about two and a half inches square every way, with a glass window occupying two thirds the upper side under a slide, with a couple of narrow slits in the wood, each side of the glass, to admit air, but too narrow for the bees to pass; the whole resting on a circular bottom a little larger than the lid of the tin box, with a sliding door in it  We were earnest to go this week, before the flowers were gone, and we feared the frosty night might make the bees slow to come forth.

After we got to the Baker Farm, to one of the open fields nearest to the tree I had marked, the first thing was to find some flowers and catch some honey-bees. We followed up the bank of the brook for some distance, but the goldenrods were all dried up there, and the asters on which we expected to find them were very scarce. By the pond-side we had no better luck, the frosts perhaps having made flowers still more scarce there. We then took the path to Clematis Brook on the north of Mt. Misery, where we found a few of the *Diplopappus linariifolius* (savory-leaved aster) and one or two small white (bushy?) asters, also *A. undulatus* and *Solidago nemoralis* rarely, on which they work in a sunny place; but there were only two or three bumblebees, wasps, and butterflies, yellow and small red, on them. We had no better luck at Clematis Brook. Not a honey-bee could we find, and we concluded that we were too late, — that the weather was too cold, and so repaired at once to the tree I had found, a hemlock two feet and a half in diameter on a side-hill a rod from the pond. I had cut my initials in the bark in the winter, for custom gives the first finder of the nest a right to the honey and to cut down the tree to get it and pay the damages,

and if he cuts his initials on it no other hunter will interfere.
Not seeing any signs of bees from the ground, one of the
party climbed the tree to where the leading stem had formerly been broken off, leaving a crotch at about eighteen
feet from the ground, and there he found a small hole into
which he thrust a stick two or three feet down the tree, and
dropped it to the bottom; and, putting in his hand, he took
out some old comb. The bees had probably died.

After eating our lunch, we set out on our return. By the
roadside at Walden, on the sunny hillside sloping to the
pond, we saw a large mass of goldenrod and aster several
rods square and comparatively fresh. Getting out of our
wagon, we found it to be resounding with the hum of bees.
(It was about 1 o'clock.) There were far more flowers than
we had seen elsewhere. Here were bees in great numbers,
both bumblebees and honey-bees, as well as butterflies and
wasps and flies. So, pouring a mixture of honey and water
into the empty comb in the tin box, and holding the lid of
the tin box in one hand and the wooden box with the slides
shut in the other, we proceeded to catch the honey-bees by
shutting them in suddenly between the lid of the tin box
and the large circular bottom of the wooden one, cutting off
the flower-stem with the edge of the lid at the same time.
Then, holding the lid still against the wooden box, we drew
the slide in the bottom and also the slide covering the window at the top, that the light might attract the bee to pass
up into the wooden box. As soon as he had done so and was
buzzing against the glass, the lower slide was closed and the
lid with the flower removed, and more bees were caught in
the same way. Then, placing the other, tin, box containing
the comb filled with honeyed water close under the wooden
one, the slide was drawn again, and the upper slide closed,
making it dark; and in about a minute they went to feeding,
as was ascertained by raising slightly the wooden box. Then

the latter was wholly removed, and they were left feeding or sucking up the honey in broad daylight. In from two to three minutes one had loaded himself and commenced leaving the box. He would buzz round it back and forth a foot or more, and then, sometimes, finding that he was too heavily loaded, alight to empty himself or clean his feet. Then, starting once more, he would begin to circle round irregularly, at first in a small circle only a foot or two in diameter, as if to examine the premises that he might know them again, till, at length, rising higher and higher and circling wider and wider and swifter and swifter, till his orbit was ten or twelve feet in diameter and as much from the ground, — though its centre might be moved to one side, — so that it was very difficult to follow him, especially if you looked against a wood or the hill, and you had to lie low to fetch him against the sky (you must operate in an open space, not in a wood); all this as if to ascertain the course to his nest; then, in a minute or less from his first starting, he darts off in a bee-line, that is, as far as I could see him, which might be eight or ten rods, looking against the sky (and you had to follow his whole career very attentively indeed to see when and where he went off at a tangent), in a waving or sinuous (right and left) line, toward his nest.

We sent forth as many as a dozen bees, which flew in about three directions, but all toward the village, or where we knew there were hives. They did not fly so almost absolutely straight as I had heard, but within three or four feet of the same course for half a dozen rods, or as far as we could see. Those belonging to one hive all had to digress to get round an apple tree. As none flew in the right direction for us, we did not attempt to line them. In less than half an hour the first returned to the box still lying on the wood-pile, — for not one of the bees on the surrounding flowers discovered it, — and so they came back, one after another, loaded themselves and departed; but now they went off with very little preliminary circling, as if assured of their course. We were furnished with little boxes of red, blue, green, yellow, and white paint, in dry powder, and with a stick we sprinkled a little of the red powder on the back of one while he was feeding, — gave him a little dab, — and it settled down amid the fuzz of his back and gave him a distinct red jacket. He went off like most of them toward some hives about three quarters of a mile distant, and we observed by the watch the time of his departure. In just twenty-two minutes red jacket came back, with enough of the powder still on his back to mark him plainly. He may have gone more than three quarters of a mile. At any rate, he had a head wind to contend with while laden. They fly swiftly and surely to their nests, never resting by the way, and I was surprised — though I had been informed of it — at the distance to which the village bees go for flowers.

### AUTOGRAPHS

*January* 1, 1853. Being at Cambridge day before yesterday, Sibley [1] told me that Agassiz told him that Harris was the greatest entomologist in the world, and gave him permission to repeat his remark. As I stood on the top of a ladder, he came along with his hand full of papers and inquired, 'Do you value autographs?' 'No, I do not,' I answered slowly and gravely. 'Oh, I didn't know but you did. I had some of Governor Dunlap,' said he, retreating.

[1] John Langdon Sibley, then assistant librarian at Harvard College under Dr. Thaddeus William Harris, whom he succeeded as librarian in 1856.

### GENIUSES

*January* 1, 1853.   After talking with Uncle Charles [1] the
other night about the worthies of this country, Webster
and the rest, as usual, considering who were geniuses and
who not, I showed him up to bed, and when I had got into
bed myself, I heard his chamber door opened, after eleven
o'clock, and he called out, in an earnest, stentorian voice,
loud enough to wake the whole house, 'Henry! was John
Quincy Adams a genius?' 'No, I think not,' was my reply.
'Well, I didn't think he was,' answered he.

### A CIDER-DRINKER

*January* 11 *and* 12, 1853.   Surveying for John L——.
He says that he saw blackbirds about a week ago.  He
says that the most snow we have had this winter (it has not
been more than one inch deep) has been only a 'robin snow,'
as it is called, i.e. a snow which does not drive off the rob-
ins. . . .
This man is continually drinking cider; thinks it corrects
some mistake in him; wishes he had a barrel of it in the
woods; if he had known he was to be out so long would have
brought a jugful; will dun Captain Hutchinson for a drink
on his way home.  This, or rum, runs in his head, if not in
his throat, all the time.  Is interested in juniper berries,
gooseberries, currants, etc., whether they will make wine;
has recipes for this.  Eats the juniper berries raw as he

[1] Charles Dunbar, brother of Thoreau's mother.

walks. Tobacco is another staff of life with him. Thinks, with others, that he has metals on his farm which the divining-rod might find, but is convertible on this point.

### LOSING ONE'S WAY AT NIGHT

*March* 29, 1853. Two or three times, when a visitor stayed into evening, and it proved a dark night, I was obliged to conduct him to the cart-path in the rear of my house and then point out to him the direction he was to pursue, and in keeping which he was to be guided rather by his feet than his eyes. One very dark night I directed thus on their way two young men who had been fishing in the pond, who would otherwise have been at a loss what course to take. They lived about a mile off, and were quite used to the woods. A day or two after, one of them told me that they wandered about the greater part of the night, close by their own premises, and did not get home till toward morning, by which time, as there were several heavy showers in the course of the night, and the leaves were very wet, they were drenched to their skins. I have heard of many going astray, even in the village streets, when the darkness was so thick that you could cut it with a knife, as the phrase is. Some who lived in the outskirts, having come to town shopping with their wagons, have been obliged to put up for the night, and gentlemen and ladies making a call have gone half a mile out of their way, feeling the sidewalk only and not knowing when they turned, and were obliged to inquire the way at the first house they discovered. Even one of the village doctors was thus lost in the heart of the village on a nocturnal mission, and spent nearly the whole night feeling the fences and the houses, being, as he said, ashamed to inquire. If one with the vision of an owl, or as in broad day-light, could have watched his motions, they would have been ludicrous indeed.

A HAVERHILL FISHERMAN

*April* 27, 1853. Haverhill.

Talked with a fisherman at the Burrough [*sic*], who was cracking and eating walnuts on a post before his hut. He said he got twenty cents a stick for sawing marked logs, which were mostly owned at Lowell, but trees that fell in and whatever was not marked belonged to them. Much went by in the ice and could not be got. They haul it in and tie it. He called it Little Concord where I lived. They got some small stuff which came from that river, and said he knew the ice, it was blue (it is not) and was turned over by the falls. The Lawrence dam breaks up the ice so now that it will not be so likely to jam below and produce a freshet. Said a thousand dollars' damage was done by a recent freshet to the farm just above, at the great bend. The wind blowing on to the shore ate it away, trees and all. In the greatest freshet he could remember, methinks about ten years ago, the water came up to his window-sill. His family took refuge on the hillside. His barn was moved and tipped over, his well filled up, and it took him, with help, a day or more to clear a passage through the ice from his door to his well. His trees were all prostrated by the ice. This was ap-parently between twenty and thirty feet above the present level. Says the railroad bridge hurts the fishing by stopping the ice and wearing away and deepening the channel near the north shore, where they fish, — draw their seines. Call it sixty rods wide, — their seines being thirty rods long, — and twenty-five feet deep in the middle.

Interesting to me are their habits and conversation who live along the shores of a great river. The shore, here some seventy or eighty feet high, is broken by gullies, more or less sandy, where water has flowed down, and the cottages rise not more than one sixth or one seventh the way up.

### A DAY WITH ALCOTT

*May* 8, 1853. I have devoted most of my day to Mr. Alcott. He is broad and genial, but indefinite; some would say feeble; forever feeling about vainly in his speech and touching nothing. But this is a very negative account of him, for he thus suggests far more than the sharp and definite practical mind. The feelers of his thought diverge, — such is the breadth of their grasp, — not converge; and in his society almost alone I can express at my leisure, with more or less success, my vaguest but most cherished fancy or thought. There are never any obstacles in the way of our meeting. He has no creed. He is not pledged to any institution. The sanest man I ever knew; the fewest crotchets, after all, has he.

It has occurred to me, while I am thinking with pleasure of our day's intercourse, 'Why should I not think aloud to you?' Having each some shingles of thought well dried, we walk and whittle them, trying our knives, and admiring the clear yellowish grain of the pumpkin pine. We wade so gently and reverently, or we pull together so smoothly, that the fishes of thought are not scared from the stream, but come and go grandly, like yonder clouds that float peacefully through the western sky. When we walk it seems as if the heavens — whose mother-o'-pearl and rainbow tints come and go, form and dissolve — and the earth had met together, and righteousness and peace had kissed each other. I have an ally against the arch-enemy. A blue-robed man dwells under the blue concave. The blue sky is a distant reflection of the azure serenity that looks out from under a human brow. We walk together like the most innocent children, going after wild pinks with case-knives.

### INCIVILITY

*May* 25, 1853.   Two young men who borrowed my boat the other day returned from the riverside through Channing's yard, quietly. It was almost the only way for them. But, as they passed out his gate, C. boorishly walked out his house behind them in his shirt-sleeves, and shut his gate again behind them as if to shut them out. It was just that sort of behavior which, if he had met with it in Italy or France, he would have complained of, whose meanness he would have condemned.

### MELVIN AND THE PINK AZALEA

*May* 31, 1853.   I am going in search of the *Azalea nudiflora.* Sophia brought home a single flower without twig or leaf from Mrs. Brooks's last evening. Mrs. Brooks, I find, has

a large twig in a vase of water, still pretty fresh, which she
says George Melvin gave to her son George. I called at his
office. He says that Melvin came in to Mr. Gourgas's office,
where he and others were sitting Saturday evening, with his
arms full and gave each a sprig, but he doesn't know where
he got it. Somebody, I heard, had seen it at Captain Jarvis's;
so I went there. I found that they had some still pretty
fresh in the house. Melvin gave it to them Saturday night,
but they did not know where he got it. A young man working at Stedman Buttrick's said it was a secret; there was
only one bush in the town; Melvin knew of it and Stedman
knew; when asked, Melvin said he got it in the swamp, or
from a bush, etc. The young man thought it grew on the
Island across the river on the Wheeler farm. I went on to
Melvin's house, though I did not expect to find him at home
at this hour, so early in the afternoon. (Saw the wood-sorrel
out, a day or two perhaps, by the way.) At length I saw his
dog by the door, and knew he was at home.

He was sitting in the shade, bareheaded, at his back door.
He had a large pailful of the azalea recently plucked and in
the shade behind his house, which he said he was going to
carry to town at evening. He had also a sprig set out. He
had been out all the forenoon and said he had got seven
pickerel, — perhaps ten. Apparently he had been drinking
and was just getting over it. At first he was a little shy about
telling me where the azalea grew, but I saw that I should get
it out of him. He dilly-dallied a little; called to his neighbor
Farmer, whom he called 'Razor,' to know if he could tell me
where that flower grew. He called it, by the way, the 'red
honeysuckle.' This was to prolong the time and make the
most of his secret. I felt pretty sure the plant was to be
found on Wheeler's land beyond the river, as the young man
had said, for I had remembered how, some weeks before this,
when I went up the Assabet after the yellow rocket, I saw

Melvin, who had just crossed with his dog, and when I landed to pluck the rocket he appeared out of the woods, said he was after a fish-pole, and asked me the name of my flower. Didn't think it was very handsome, — 'not so handsome as the honeysuckle, is it?' And now I knew it was his 'red honeysuckle,' and not the columbine, he meant. Well, I told him he had better tell me where it was: I was a botanist and ought to know. But he thought I couldn't possibly find it by his directions. I told him he'd better tell me and have the glory of it, for I should surely find it if he didn't; I'd got a clue to it, and shouldn't give it up. I should go over the river for it. I could smell it a good way, you know. He thought I could smell it half a mile, and he wondered that I hadn't stumbled on it, or Channing. Channing, he said, came close by it once, when it was in flower. He thought he'd surely find it then; but he didn't, and he said nothing to him.

He told me he found it about ten years ago, and he went to it every year. It blossomed at the old election time, and he thought it 'the handsomest flower that grows.' Yarrow just out.

In the meanwhile, Farmer, who was hoeing, came up to the wall, and we fell into a talk about Dodge's Brook, which runs through his farm. A man in Cambridge, he said, had recently written to Mr. Monroe about it, but he didn't know why. All he knew about the brook was that he had seen it dry and then again, after a week of dry weather in which no rain fell, it would be full again, and either the writer or Monroe said there were only two such brooks in all North America. One of its sources — he thought the principal one — was in his land. We all went to it. It was in a meadow, — rather a dry one, once a swamp. He said it never ceased to flow at the head now, since he dug it out, and never froze there. He ran a pole down eight or nine feet into the mud to show me the depth. He had minnows there in a large deep pool, and cast an insect into the water, which they presently rose to and swallowed. Fifteen years ago he dug it out nine feet deep and found spruce logs as big as his leg, which the beavers had gnawed, with the marks of their teeth very distinct upon them; but they soon crumbled away on coming to the air. Melvin, meanwhile, was telling me of a pair of geese he had seen which were breeding in the Bedford Swamp. He had seen them within a day. Last year he got a large brood (11?) of black ducks there.

We went on down the brook, — Melvin and I and his dog, — and crossed the river in his boat, and he conducted me to where the *Azalea nudiflora* grew, — it was a little past its prime, perhaps, — and showed me how near Channing came. ('You won't tell him what I said; will you?' said he.) I offered to pay him for his trouble, but he wouldn't take anything. He had just as lief I'd know as not. He thought it first came out last Wednesday, on the 25th.

## MELVIN AND HIS GUN

*May* 31, 1853. Jarvis tells me that Stedman Buttrick once hired Melvin to work for him on condition that he should not take his gun into the field, but he had known him to do so when Buttrick was away and earn two or three dollars with his game beside his day's work, but of course the last was neglected.

## THE FARMER'S HORN

*June* 1, 1853. I hear now, at five o'clock, from this hill, a farmer's horn calling his hands in from the field to an early tea. Heard afar by the walker, over the woods at this hour or at noon, bursting upon the stillness of the air, putting life into some portion of the horizon, this is one of the most suggestive and pleasing of the country sounds produced by man. I know not how far it is peculiar to New England or the United States. I hear two or three prolonged blasts, as I am walking alone some sultry noon in midst of the still woods, — a sound which I know to be produced by human breath, the most sonorous parts of which alone reach me, — and I see in my mind the hired men and master dropping the implements of their labor in the field and wending their way with a sober satisfaction toward the house; I see the well-sweep rise and fall; I see the preparatory ablutions and the table laden with the smoking meal. It is a significant hum in a distant part of the hive. Often it tells me the time of day.

## A HIRED GIRL'S WORK

*June* 9, 1853. I was amused by the account which Mary, the Irish girl who left us the other day, gave of her experience at —— ——, the milkman's, in the north part of the town. She said that twenty-two lodged in the house the first night, including two pig men, that Mr. —— kept ten men, had six children and a deaf wife, and one of the men had his wife with him, who helped sew, beside taking care of her own child. Also all the cooking and washing for his father and mother, who live in another house and whom he is bound to carry through, is done in his house, and she, Mary, was the only girl they hired; and the workmen were called up at four by an alarm clock which was set a quarter of an hour ahead of the clock downstairs, — and that more than as much ahead of the town clock, — and she was on her feet from that hour till nine at night. Each man had two pairs of overalls in the wash, and the cans to be scalded were countless. Having got through washing the breakfast dishes by a quarter before twelve, Sunday noon, by ——'s time, she left, no more to return. He had told her that the work was easy, that girls had lived with him to recover their health, and then went away to be married. He is regarded as one of the most enterprising and thrifty farmers in the county, and takes the premiums of the Agricultural Society. He probably exacts too much of his hands.

## A LURKER IN THE WOODS

*June* 14, 1853. C. says he saw a 'lurker' yesterday in the woods on the Marlborough road. He heard a distressing noise like a man sneezing but long continued, but at length found it was a man wheezing. He was oldish and grizzled, the stumps of his grizzled beard about an inch long, and his clothes in the worst possible condition, — a wretched-looking creature, an escaped convict hiding in the woods, perhaps. He appeared holding on to his paunch, and wheezing as if it would kill him. He appeared to have come straight through the swamp, and — what was most interesting about him, and proved him to be a lurker of the first class, — one of our party, as C. said, — he kept straight through a field of rye which was fully grown, not regarding it in the least; and, though C. tried to conceal himself on the edge of the rye, fearing to hurt his feelings if the man should mistake him for the proprietor, yet they met, and the lurker, giving him a short bow, disappeared in the woods on the opposite side of the road. He went through everything.

## THREE REFORMERS

*June* 17, 1853. Here have been three ultra-reformers, lecturers on Slavery, Temperance, the Church, etc., in and about our house and Mrs. Brooks's the last three or four days, — A. D. Foss, once a Baptist minister in Hopkinton, N. H.; Loring Moody, a sort of travelling pattern-working chaplain; and H. C. Wright, who shocks all the old women

# PLATE VI

*Thoreau and the Three Reformers*

with his infidel writings. Though Foss was a stranger to the others, you would have thought them old and familiar cronies. (They happened here together by accident.) They addressed each other constantly by their Christian names, and rubbed you continually with the greasy cheeks of their kindness. They would not keep their distance, but cuddle up and lie spoon-fashion with you, no matter how hot the weather nor how narrow the bed, — chiefly ——.[1] I was awfully pestered with his benignity; feared I should get greased all over with it past restoration; tried to keep some starch in my clothes. He wrote a book called 'A Kiss for a Blow,' and he behaved as if there were no alternative between these, or as if I had given him a blow. I would have preferred the blow, but he was bent on giving me the kiss, when there was neither quarrel nor agreement between us. I wanted that he should straighten his back, smooth out those ogling wrinkles of benignity about his eyes, and, with a healthy reserve, pronounce something in a downright manner. It was difficult to keep clear of his slimy benignity, with which he sought to cover you before he swallowed you and took you fairly into his bowels. It would have been far worse than the fate of Jonah. I do not wish to get any nearer to a man's bowels than usual. They lick you as a cow her calf. They would fain wrap you about with their bowels. —— addressed me as 'Henry' within one minute from the time I first laid eyes on him, and when I spoke, he said with drawling, sultry sympathy, 'Henry, I know all you would say; I understand you perfectly; you need not explain anything to me;' and to another, 'I am going to dive into Henry's inmost depths.' I said, 'I trust you will not strike your head

[1] In the original journal Thoreau had crossed out the 'chiefly' and substituted 'wholly' in pencil. It was Wright who was the author of *A Kiss for a Blow* — Henry Clarke Wright (1797–1870), a lecturer on slavery, peace, socialism, spiritism, etc.

against the bottom.' He could tell in a dark room, with his eyes blinded and in perfect stillness, if there was one there whom he loved. One of the most attractive things about the flowers is their beautiful reserve. The truly beautiful and noble puts its lover, as it were, at an infinite distance, while it attracts him more strongly than ever. I do not like the men who come so near me with their bowels. It is the most disagreeable kind of snare to be caught in. Men's bowels are far more slimy than their brains. They must be ascetics indeed who approach you by this side. What a relief to have heard the ring of one healthy reserved tone! With such a forgiving disposition, as if he were all the while forgiving you for existing. Considering our condition or *habit* of soul, — maybe corpulent and asthmatic, — maybe dying of atrophy, with all our bones sticking out, — is it kindness to embrace a man? They lay their sweaty hand on your shoulder, or your knee, to magnetize you.

### GRANNY KNOTS

*July* 25, 1853. I have for years had a great deal of trouble with my shoe-strings, because they get untied continually. They are leather, rolled and tied in a hard knot. But some days I could hardly go twenty rods before I was obliged to stop and stoop to tie my shoes. My companion and I speculated on the distance to which one tying would carry you, — the length of a shoe-tie, — and we thought it nearly as appreciable and certainly a more simple and natural measure of distance than a stadium, or league, or mile. Ever and anon we raised our feet on whatever fence or wall or rock or stump we chanced to be passing, and drew the strings once more, pulling as hard as we could. It was very vexatious, when passing through low scrubby bushes, to become conscious that the strings were already getting loose again before we had fairly started. What should we have done if pursued by a tribe of Indians? My companion sometimes went without strings altogether, but that loose way of proceeding was not to be thought of by me. One shoemaker sold us shoe-strings made of the hide of a South American jackass, which he recommended; or rather he gave them to us and added their price to that of the shoes we bought of him. But I could not see that these were any better than the old. I wondered if anybody had exhibited a better article at the World's Fair, and whether England did not bear the palm from America in this respect. I thought of strings with recurved prickles and various other remedies myself. At last the other day it occurred to me that I would try an experiment, and, instead of tying two simple knots one over the other the same way, putting the end which fell to the right over each time, that I would reverse the process, and put it under the other. Greatly to my satisfaction, the experiment was perfectly successful, and from that time my shoe-strings have given me no trouble, except sometimes in untying them at night.

On telling this to others I learned that I had been all the while tying what is called a granny's knot, for I had never been taught to tie any other, as sailors' children are; but now I had blundered into a square knot, I think they called it, or two running slip-nooses. Should not all children be taught this accomplishment, and an hour, perchance, of their childhood be devoted to instruction in tying knots?

## ALCOTT AND THE ABOLITION SOCIETY

*August* 10, 1853.   Alcott spent the day with me yesterday.
He spent the day before with Emerson.  He observed that
he had got his wine and now he had come after his venison.
Such was the compliment he paid me.  The question of a
livelihood was troubling him.  He knew of nothing which he
could do for which men would pay him.  He could not com-
pete with the Irish in cradling grain.  His early education
had not fitted him for a clerkship.  He had offered his serv-
ices to the Abolition Society, to go about the country and
speak for freedom as their agent, but they declined him.
This is very much to their discredit; they should have been
forward to secure him.  Such a connection with him would
confer unexpected dignity on their enterprise.  But they cannot tolerate a man who stands by a head above them.  They
are as bad — Garrison and Phillips, etc. — as the overseers
and faculty of Harvard College.  They require a man who
will train well *under* them.  Consequently they have not in
their employ any but small men, — trainers.

### CARRYING A SUBSCRIPTION PAPER

*October* 12, 1853.   To-day I have had the experience of bor-
rowing money for a poor Irishman who wishes to get his
family to this country.[1]  One will never know his neighbors
till he has carried a subscription paper among them.  Ah!
it reveals many and sad facts to stand in this relation to

[1] See page 102 and note.

them. To hear the selfish and cowardly excuses some make, — that *if* they help any they must help the Irishman who lives with them, — and him they are sure never to help! Others, with whom public opinion weighs, will think of it, trusting you never will raise the sum and so they will not be called on again; who give stingily after all. What a satire in the fact that you are much more inclined to call on a certain slighted and so-called crazy woman in moderate circumstances rather than on the president of the bank! But some are generous and save the town from the distinction which threatened it, and *some* even who do not lend, plainly would if they could.

### JOHN GOODWIN, FISHERMAN

*October* 22, 1853. Yesterday, toward night, gave Sophia and mother a sail as far as the Battle-Ground. One-eyed John Goodwin, the fisherman, was loading into a hand-cart and conveying home the piles of driftwood which of late he had collected with his boat. It was a beautiful evening, and a clear amber sunset lit up all the eastern shores; and that man's employment, so simple and direct, — though he is regarded by most as a vicious character, — whose whole motive was so easy to fathom, — thus to obtain his winter's wood, — charmed me unspeakably. So much do we love actions that are simple. They are all poetic. We, too, would fain be so employed. . . .

Goodwin is a most constant fisherman. He must well know the taste of pickerel by this time. He will fish, I would not venture to say how many days in succession. When I can remember to have seen him fishing almost daily for some time, if it rains, I am surprised on looking out to see him slowly wending his way to the river in his oilcloth coat, with his basket and pole. I saw him the other day fishing in the middle of the stream, the day after I had seen him fishing on the shore, while by a kind of magic I sailed by him; and he said he was catching minnow for bait in the winter. When I was twenty rods off, he held up a pickerel that weighed two and a half pounds, which he had forgot to show me before, and the next morning, as he afterward told me, he caught one that weighed three pounds. If it is ever necessary to appoint a committee on fish-ponds and pickerel, let him be one of them. Surely he is tenacious of life, hard to scale.

### DEGREES OF MEANNESS

*November* 1, 1853. About three weeks ago my indignation was roused by hearing that one of my townsmen, notorious for meanness, was endeavoring to get and keep a premium of four dollars which a poor Irish laborer [1] whom he hired had gained by fifteen minutes' spading at our Agricultural Fair. To-night a free colored woman is lodging at our house, whose errand to the North is to get money to buy her husband, who is a slave to one Moore in Norfolk, Virginia. She persuaded Moore, though not a kind master, to buy him that he might not be sold further South. Moore paid six

---

[1] Mr. Sanborn tells us in his *Life of Henry David Thoreau* that this was Michael Flannery (see page 435) and that this treatment 'so incensed Thoreau that he collected the sum among his neighbors and paid it to Mike, whom the Thoreaus ever afterward befriended.' He goes on to say: 'When Sophia [Thoreau] left Concord to live and die in Bangor, among her cousins, she gave me a small note of hand, which Flannery had signed for money lent him in some pinch, with instructions to receive payment if he was able to pay, but in any case to give him up the note, which I did. This is a sample, one of many, of the relations of the Thoreaus with the poor.' See *ante*, page 100.

hundred dollars for him, but asks her eight hundred. My most natural reflection was that he was even meaner than my townsman. As mean as a slaveholder!

## THE PRICE OF CRANBERRIES

*November* 20, 1853. I once came near speculating in cranberries. Being put to it to raise the wind to pay for 'A Week on the Concord and Merrimack Rivers,' and having occasion to go to New York to peddle some pencils which I had made, as I passed through Boston I went to Quincy Market and inquired the price of cranberries. The dealers took me down cellar, asked if I wanted wet or dry, and showed me them. I gave them to understand that I might want an indefinite quantity. It made a slight sensation among them and for aught I know raised the price of the berry for a time. I then visited various New York packets and was told what would be the freight, on deck and in the hold, and one skipper was very anxious for my freight. When I got to New York, I again visited the markets as a purchaser, and 'the best of Eastern Cranberries' were offered me by the barrel at a cheaper rate than I could buy them in Boston. I was obliged to manufacture a thousand dollars' worth of pencils and slowly dispose of and finally sacrifice them, in order to pay an assumed debt of a hundred dollars.

### THE STORY OF A MAD DOG

*November* 29, 1853.   On Saturday, the 26th, a dog on whose collar the words 'Milton Hill,' or equivalent ones, were engraved ran through the town, having, as the story went, bitten a boy in Lincoln.  He bit several dogs in this town and was finally shot.  Some of the dogs bitten have been killed, and rumor now says that the boy died yesterday.  People are considerably alarmed.  Some years ago a boy in Lincoln was bitten by a raccoon and died of hydrophobia.  I observed to Minott to-night that I did not think that our doctors knew how to cure this disease, but he said they could cure it, he had seen a man bitten who was cured.  The story is worth telling, for it shows how much trouble the passage of one mad dog through the town may produce.

It was when he was a boy and lived down below the old Ben Prescott house, over the cellar-hole on what is now Hawthorne's land.  The first he remembers a couple of men had got poles and were punching at a strange dog toward night under a barn in that neighborhood.  The dog, which was speckled and not very large, would growl and bite the pole, and they ran a good deal of risk, but they did not know that he was mad.  At length they routed him, and he took to the road and came on towards town, and Minott, keeping his distance, followed on behind.  When the dog got to the old Ben Prescott place, he turned up into the yard, where there were a couple of turkeys, drove them into a corner, bit off the head of one, and carried the body off across the road into the meadow opposite.  They then raised the cry of 'Mad dog.'  He saw his mother and Aunt Prescott, two old ladies, coming down the road, while the dog was running the other way in the meadow, and he shouted to them to take

care of themselves, for that dog was mad. The dog soon re-
entered the road at some bars and held on toward town.
Minott next saw Harry Hooper coming down the road after
his cows, and he shouted to him to look out, for the dog was
mad, but Harry, who was in the middle of the road, spread
his arms out, one on each side, and, being short, the dog
leaped right upon his open breast and made a pass at his
throat, but missed it, though it frightened him a good deal;
and Minott, coming up, exclaimed, 'Why, you're crazy,
Harry; if he'd 'a' bitten ye, 'twould 'a' killed ye.' When he
got up as far as the red house or Curtis place, the dog was
about in the middle of the road, and a large and stout old
gentleman by the name of Fay, dressed in small-clothes, was
coming down on the sidewalk. M. shouted to him also to
take care of himself, for the dog was mad, and Fay said
afterward that he heard him but he had always supposed
that a mad dog wouldn't turn out for anything; but when
this dog was nearly abreast of him, he suddenly inclined
toward him, and then again inclined still more, and seized
him by the left leg just below the knee, and Fay, giving him
a kick with the other leg, tripped himself up; and when he
was down, the dog bit him in the right leg in the same place.
Being by this time well frightened, and fearing that he would
spring at his throat next, Fay seized the dog himself by his
throat and held him fast, and called lustily for somebody
to come and kill him. A man by the name of Lewis rushed
out of the red house with an old axe and began to tap on the
dog's nose with it, but he was afraid to strike harder, for
Fay told him not to hit him. Minott saw it all, but still kept
his distance. Suddenly Fay, not knowing what he did, let go,
and the man, giving the dog a blow across the back, ran
into the house; but, it being a dull meat axe, the dog trotted
along, still toward town.

He turned and went round the pond by Bowers's and,

going down to the brook by the roadside, lapped some water. Just then, Peter coming over the bridge, the dog reared up and growled at him, and he, seeing that he was mad, made haste through the bars out of his way and cut across the fields to Reuben Brown's. The dog went on, it being now between sundown and dark, to Peter Wheeler's, and bit two cows, which afterward died of hydrophobia, and next he went to where Nathan Stow now lives, and bit a goose in the wing, and so he kept on through the town. The next that was heard of him, Black Cato, that lived at the Lee place, now Sam Wheeler's, on the river, was waked up about midnight by a noise among the pigs, and, having got up, he took a club and went out to see what was the matter. Looking over into the pen, this dog reared up at him, and he knocked him back into it, and, jumping over, mauled him till he thought he was dead and then tossed him out. In the morning he thought he would go out and see whose dog he had killed, but lo! he had picked himself up, and there was no dog to be found.

Cato was going out into the woods chopping that day, and as he was getting over a wall lined with brush, the same dog reared up at him once more, but this time, having heard of the mad dog, he was frightened and ran; but still the dog came on, and once or twice he knocked him aside with a large stone, till at length, the dog coming close to him, he gave him a blow which killed him; and lest he should run away again, he cut off his head and threw both head and body into the river.

In the meanwhile Fay went home (to the Dr. Heywood house), drank some spirit, then went straight over to Dr. Heywood's office and stayed there and was doctored by him for three weeks. The doctor cut out the mangled flesh and made various applications, and Fay cried like a baby, but he never experienced any further ill effects from the bite.

EMERSON AND HIS CALF

*December* 8, 1853. I was amused by R. W. E.'s telling me
that he drove his own calf out of the yard, as it was coming in
with the cow, not knowing it to be his own, a drove going by
at the time.

SURVEYING AND LECTURING

*December* 22, 1853. Surveying the last three days. They
have not yielded much that I am aware of. All I find is old
boundmarks, and the slowness and dullness of farmers re-

confirmed. They even complain that I walk too fast for them. Their legs have become stiff from toil. This coarse and hurried outdoor work compels me to live grossly or be inattentive to my diet; that is the worst of it. Like work, like diet; that, I find, is the rule. Left to my chosen pursuits, I should never drink tea nor coffee, nor eat meat. The diet of any class or generation is the natural result of its employment and locality. It is remarkable how unprofitable it is for the most part to talk with farmers. They commonly stand on their good behavior and attempt to moralize or philosophize in a serious conversation. Sportsmen and loafers are better company. For society a man must not be too *good* or well-disposed, to spoil his natural disposition. The bad are frequently good enough to let you see how bad they are, but the good as frequently endeavor to get between you and themselves.

I have dined out five times and tea'd once within a week.[1] Four times there was tea on the dinner-table, always meat, but once baked beans, always pie, but no puddings. I suspect tea has taken the place of cider with farmers. I am reminded of Haydon the painter's experience when he went about painting the nobility. I go about to the houses of the farmers and squires in like manner. This is my portrait-painting, — when I would fain be employed on higher subjects. I have offered myself much more earnestly as a lecturer than a surveyor. Yet I do not get any employment as a lecturer; was not invited to lecture once last winter, and only once (without pay) this winter. But I can get surveying enough, which a hundred others in this county can do as well as I, though it is not boasting much to say that a hundred others in New England cannot lecture as well as I on my themes.

[1] Dinner was, of course, the mid-day meal, and 'tea' was supper.

## THERIEN, THE WOODCHOPPER

*December* 24, 1853. Saw Therien yesterday afternoon chopping for Jacob Baker in the rain. I heard his axe half a mile off, and also saw the smoke of his fire, which I mistook for a part of the mist which was drifting about. I asked him where he boarded. At Shannon's. He asked the price of board and said I was a *grass* boarder, i.e. not a regular one. Asked him what time he started in the morning. The sun was up when he got out of the house that morning. He heard Flint's Pond whooping like cannon the moment he opened the door, but sometimes he could see stars after he got to his chopping-ground. He was working with his coat off in the rain. He said he often saw gray squirrels running about and jumping from tree to tree. There was a large nest of leaves close by. That morning he saw a large bird of some kind. He took a French paper to keep himself in practice, — not for news; he said he didn't want news. He had got twenty-three or twenty-four of them, had got them bound and paid a dollar for it, and would like to have me see it. He hadn't read it half; there was a great deal of reading in it, by gorry. He wanted me to tell him the meaning of some of the hard words. How much had he cut? He wasn't a-going to kill himself. He had got money enough. He cut enough to earn his board. A man could not do much more in the winter. He used the dry twigs on the trees to start his fire with, and some shavings which he brought in his pocket. He frequently found some fire still in the morning. He laid his axe by a log and placed another log the other side of it. I said he might have to dig it out of a snowdrift, but he thought it would not snow. Described a large hawk killed at Smith's (which had eaten some hens); its legs 'as yellow as a sovereign;' ap-

parently a goshawk. He has also his beetle and wedges and
whetstone.

### AN IRISHMAN SEEKING WORK

*December* 26, 1853. Was overtaken by an Irishman seeking
work. I asked him if he could chop wood. He said he was
not long in this country; that he could cut one side of a tree
well enough, but he had not learned to change hands and
cut the other without going around it, — what we call crossing the carf. They get very small wages at this season of the
year; almost give up the ghost in the effort to keep soul and
body together. He left me on the run to find a new master.

### A PRIZE FARMER

*December* 28, 1853. E. W——, who got the premium on
farms this year, keeps twenty-eight cows, which are milked
before breakfast, or 6 o'clock, his hired men rising at 4.30
A.M.; but he gives them none of the milk in their coffee.

### THE PHILOSOPHICAL WOODCHOPPER

*December* 29, 1853. I asked Therien yesterday if he was
satisfied with himself. I was trying to get a *point d'appui*
within him, a shelf to spring an arch from, to suggest some

employment and aim for life. 'Satisfied!' said he; 'some men are satisfied with one thing, and some with another, by George. One man, perhaps, if he has got enough, will be satisfied to sit all day with his back to the fire and his belly to the table; that will satisfy him, by gorry.' When I met him the other day, he asked me if I had made any improvement. Yet I could never by any manœuvring get him to take what is called a spiritual view of things, of life. He allowed that study and education was a good thing, but for him it was too late. He only thought of its expediency; nothing answering to what many call their aspirations. He was humble, if he can be called humble who never aspires.

He cut his trees very low, close to the ground, because the sprouts that came from such stumps were better. Perhaps he distinguished between the red and scarlet oak; one had a pale inner bark, the other a darker or more reddish one. Without the least effort he could defend prevailing institutions which affected him, better than any philosopher, because he implicitly accepted them and knew their whole value. He gave the true reason for their prevalence, because speculation had never suggested to him any other. Looking round among the trees, he said he could enjoy himself in the woods chopping alone in a winter day; he wanted no better sport. The trees were frozen, — had been sometimes, — but would frequently thaw again during the day. Split easier for it, but did not chop better.

The woodchopper to-day is the same man that Homer refers to, and his work the same. He, no doubt, had his beetle and wedge and whetstone then, carried his dinner in a pail or basket, and his liquor in a bottle, and caught his woodchucks, and cut and corded, the same.

## WILLIAM TAPPAN

*January* 9, 1854. T.[1] has a singularly elastic step. He will run through the snow, lifting his knees like a child who enjoys the motion. When he slumped once through to water and called my attention to it, with an indescribable flash of his eye, he reminded me forcibly of Hawthorne's little son Julian. He uses the greatest economy in speech of any man I know. Speaks low, beside, and without emphasis; in monosyllables. I cannot guess what the word was for a long time. His language is different from the Algonquin.

### TAPPAN'S SPEECH

*January* 10, 1854. With Tappan, his speech is frequently so frugal and reserved, in monosyllables not fairly uttered clear of his thought, that I doubt if he did not cough merely, or let it pass for such, instead of asking what he said or meant, for fear it might turn out that he coughed merely.

Channing showed me last night on a map where, as he said, he 'used to walk' in Rome. He was there sixteen days.

[1] William Tappan, of New York, with whom Thoreau became acquainted during his stay with William Emerson on Staten Island in 1843. He was the son of Lewis Tappan, who founded the first mercantile agency in the United States. He himself was a contributor to the *Dial*.

## AUCTIONS

*January* 27, 1854. Attended the auction of Deacon Brown's effects a little while to-day, — a great proportion of old traps, rubbish, or trumpery, which began to accumulate in his father's day, and now, after lying half a century in his garret and other dust-holes, is not burned, but surviving neighbors collect and view it, and buy it, and carefully transport it to their garrets and dust-holes, to lie there till their estates are settled, when it will start again. Among his effects was a dried tapeworm and various articles too numerous and worthless to mention. A pair of old snow-shoes is almost regularly sold on these occasions, though none of this generation has seen them worn here.

### DEACON BROWN'S ANN

*February* 8, 1854. Ann, the Irishwoman who has lived with Deacon Brown so long, says that when he had taken to his bed with his last illness, she was startled by his calling, 'Ann, Ann,' 'the bitterest Ann that you ever heard,' and that was the beginning of his last illness.

## MINOTT AND SPRING

*March* 5, 1854.  Channing, talking with Minott the other day about his health, said, 'I suppose you'd like to die now.' 'No,' said Minott, 'I've toughed it through the winter, and I want to stay and hear the bluebirds once more.'

## MR. HOAR

*April* 5, 1854.  I rode with my employer [1] a dozen miles to-day, keeping a profound silence almost all the way as the most simple and natural course.  I treated him simply as if he had bronchitis and could not speak, just as I would a sick man, a crazy man, or an idiot.  The disease was only an unconquerable stiffness in a well-meaning and sensible man.

## MUSKRAT-SHOOTING

*May* 1, 1854.  I have seen Goodwin and Haynes all day hunting muskrats and ducks, stealthily paddling along the riverside or by the willows and button-bushes, now the river is so high, and shooting any rat that may expose himself. In one instance a rat they had wounded looked exactly like

[1] Samuel Hoar, for whom Thoreau was doing some surveying.  He was a leading citizen of Concord and father of Judge Ebenezer Rockwood Hoar and Senator George F. Hoar.

PLATE VII

*The Muskrat-Hunters, Goodwin and Haynes*

the end of an old rider stripped of bark, as it lay just on the surface close to the shore within a few feet of them. Haynes would not at first believe it a muskrat only six or eight feet off, and the dog could not find it. How pitiful a man looks about this sport! Haynes reminded me of the Penobscots. . . .

*May* 6, 1854. Remembering my voyage of May 1st, and Goodwin and Haynes hunting, you might have passed up and down the river three or four miles and yet not have seen one muskrat, yet they killed six at least. One in stern paddling slowly along, while the other sat with his gun ready cocked and the dog erect in the prow, all eyes constantly scanning the surface amid the button-bushes and willows, for the rats are not easy to distinguish from a bunch of dried grass or a stick. Suddenly one is seen resting on his perch, and crack goes the gun, and over the dog instantly goes to fetch him. These men represent a class which probably always exists, even in the most civilized community, and allies it to the most savage. Goodwin said in the morning that he was laying stone, but it was so muddy on account of the rain that he told Haynes he would like to take a cruise out.

## THE MEADOW-HAYING

*August* 5, 1854. Now Lee and his men are returning to their meadow-haying after dinner, and stop at the well under the black oak in the field. I too repair to the well when they are gone, and taste the flavor of black strap on the bucket's edge. As I return down-stream, I see the haymakers now raking with hand or horse rakes into long rows or loading, one on the load placing it and treading it down, while others fork it up to him; and others are gleaning with rakes after the forkers. All farmers are anxious to get their meadow-hay as soon as possible for fear the river will rise. On the 2d, Hagar told me he had done all his haying, having little or no meadow, and now the chief business was to kill weeds in the orchard, etc. Formerly they used to think they had nothing to do when the haying was done and might go a-fishing for three weeks.

## A TALK WITH GARFIELD

*September* 8, 1854. Talked with Garfield, who was fishing off his shore. By the way, that shore might be named from him, for he is the genius of it, and is almost the only man I ever see on that part of the river. He says that the two turtles, of one of which I have the shell, weighed together eighty-nine pounds. He saw one when he was a boy, which his father caught in Fair Haven Pond, which several who saw it thought would have weighed sixty pounds. That the biggest story he could tell. Referred to the year not long since when so many were found dead. There was one rotting right on that shore where we were, 'as big as a tray.' Once, he and another man were digging a ditch in a meadow in Waltham. (He thought it was the last of September or first of October — and that we did not see them put their heads out much later than this.) They found two mud turtles three feet beneath the surface and no hole visible by which they entered. They laid them out on the grass, but when they went to look for them again, one was lost and the other had buried himself in the meadow all but the tip of his tail.

He heard some years ago a large flock of brant go over

'yelling' very loud, flying low and in an irregular dense flock like pigeons. He says the east shore of Fair Haven under the Hill is covered with heron-tracks. One of his boys had seen marks where an otter had slid and eaten fish near the mouth of Pole Brook (my Bidens Brook). Remembered old people saying that this river used to be a great hunting-place a hundred years ago or more. A still stream with meadows, and the deer used to come out on it. Had heard an old Mr. Hosmer, who lived where E. Conant does, say that he had shot three dozen muskrats at one shot at Birch Island (the island at mouth of Fair Haven Pond).

His father caught the great turtle while fishing and sent him up to the house on Baker's farm where a Jones lived, to get an axe to cut his head off. There were two or three men — Luke Potter, who lived where Hayden does, for one — playing cards, and when they learned what he wanted the axe for, they came down to the shore to see him, and they judged that he would weigh sixty pounds. Two or three years ago he saw one caught that weighed forty-two pounds.

PIRATE MONEY

*November* 5, 1854. Passing the mouth of John Hosmer's hollow near the river, was hailed by him and Anthony Wright, sitting there, to come and see where they had dug for money. There was a hole six feet square and as many deep, and the sand was heaped about over a rod square. Hosmer said that it was dug two or three weeks before, that three men came in a chaise and dug it in the night. They were seen about there by day. Somebody dug near there in June, and then they covered up the hole again. He said they

had been digging thereabouts from time to time for a hundred years. I asked him why. He said that Dr. Lee, who lived where Joe Barrett did, told him that old Mr. Wood, who lived in a house very near his (Hosmer's), told him that, one night in Captain Kidd's day, three pirates came to his house with a pair of old-fashioned deer-skin breeches, both legs full of coin, and asked leave to bury it in his cellar. He was afraid, and refused them. They then asked for some earthen pots and shovels and a lanthorn, which he let them have. A woman in the house followed the pirates at a distance down the next hollow on the south, and saw them go along the meadow-side and turn up this hollow, and then, being alone and afraid, she returned. Soon after the men returned with the tools and an old-fashioned hat full of the coin (holding about a quart), which they gave to Wood.

He, being afraid, buried it in his cellar, but afterward, becoming a poor man, dug it up and used it. A bailiff made some inquiry hereabouts after the pirates.

Hosmer said that one thing which confirmed the diggers in their belief was the fact that when he was a little boy, plowing one day with his father on the hillside, they found three old-fashioned bottles bottom upward but empty under the plow. Somebody consulted Moll Pitcher, who directed to dig at a certain distance from an apple tree on a line with the bottles, and then they would find the treasure.

### SEEING NEW YORK [1]

*November* 22, 1854. Went to Crystal Palace; admired the houses on Fifth Avenue, the specimens of coal at the Palace, one fifty feet thick as it was cut from the mine, in the form of a square column, iron and copper ore, etc. Saw sculptures and paintings innumerable, and armor from the Tower of London, some of the Eighth Century. Saw Greeley; Snow, the commercial editor of the *Tribune*; Solon Robinson; Fry, the musical critic, etc.; and others. Greeley carried me to the new opera-house, where I heard Grisi and her troupe. First, at Barnum's Museum, I saw the camelopards, said to be one eighteen the other sixteen feet high. I should say the highest stood about fifteen feet high at most (twelve or thirteen ordinarily). The body was only about five feet long. Why has it horns, but for ornament? Looked through his diorama, and found the houses all over the world much alike. Greeley appeared to know and be known by everybody;

[1] Thoreau was staying over in New York on his way back from a day's visit to Philadelphia, where he probably delivered a lecture.

was admitted free to the opera, and we were led by a page to
various parts of the house at different times.

## LECTURING

*December* 6, 1854. After lecturing twice this winter I feel
that I am in danger of cheapening myself by trying to become a successful lecturer, *i. e.*, to interest my audiences.[1]
I am disappointed to find that most that I am and value
myself for is lost, or worse than lost, on my audience. I fail
to get even the attention of the mass. I should suit them
better if I suited myself less. I feel that the public demand
an average man, — average thoughts and manners, — not
originality, nor even absolute excellence. You cannot interest them except as you are like them and sympathize
with them. I would rather that my audience come to me
than that I should go to them, and so they be sifted; *i. e.*, I
would rather write books than lectures. That is fine, this
coarse. To read to a promiscuous audience who are at your
mercy the fine thoughts you solaced yourself with far away
is as violent as to fatten geese by cramming, and in this
case they do not get fatter.

[1] This was written in Providence, where he had lectured that day or evening
in the 'depot.'

### CHANNING AS A SKATER

*December* 20, 1854. P. M. — Skated to Fair Haven with C.
C.'s skates are not the best, and beside he is far from an
easy skater, so that, as he said, it was killing work for him.
Time and again the perspiration actually dropped from his
forehead on to the ice, and it froze in long icicles on his beard.
Yet he kept up his spirits and his fun, said he had seen much
more suffering than I, etc., etc.

### THERIEN'S BOARDING-PLACES

*February* 14, 1855. I said to Therien, 'You didn't live at
Smith's last summer. Where did you live? At Baker's?'
'Yes,' said he. 'Well, is that a good place?' 'Oh, yes.'
'Is that a better place than Smith's?' 'Oh, a change of pas-
ture makes a fatter calf.'

### DADDY DUDLEY

*October* 18, 1855. When I was surveying for Legross, as we
went to our work in the morning, we passed by the Dudley
family tomb, and Legross remarked to me, all in good faith,
'Wouldn't you like to see old Daddy Dudley? He lies in
there. I'll get the keys if you'd like. I sometimes go in and
look at him.'

## AN IRISHWOMAN'S FAGOTS

*October* 19, 1855. I see Mrs. Riordan and her little boy coming out of the woods with their bundles of fagots on their backs. It is surprising what great bundles of wood an Irishwoman will contrive to carry. I confess that though I could carry one I should hardly think of making such a bundle of them. They are first regularly tied up, and then carried on the back by a rope, — somewhat like the Indian women and their straps. There is a strange similarity; and the little boy carries his bundle proportionally large. The sticks about four feet long. They make haste to deposit their loads before I see them, for they do not know how pleasant a sight it is to me. The Irishwoman does the squaw's part in many respects. Riordan also buys the old railroad sleepers at three dollars a hundred, but they are much decayed and full of sand.

## BELLEW AND FOURIERISM

*October* 19, 1855. Talking with Bellew [1] this evening about Fourierism and communities, I said that I suspected any enterprise in which two were engaged together. 'But,' said he, 'it is difficult to make a stick stand unless you slant two or more against it.' 'Oh, no,' answered I, 'you may split its lower end into three, or drive it single into the ground, which is the best way; but most men, when they start on a new enterprise, not only figuratively, but really, *pull up stakes.*

[1] Frank H. T. Bellew (1828–88), of New York, well known as a caricaturist.

When the sticks prop one another, none, or only one stands erect.'

He showed me a sketch of Wachusett. Spoke of his life in Paris, etc. I asked him if he had ever visited the Alps and sketched there. He said he had not. Had he been to the White Mountains? 'No,' he answered, 'the highest mountains I have ever seen were the Himalayas, though I was only two years old then.' It seems that he was born in that neighborhood.

He complains that the Americans have attained to bad luxuries, but have no comforts.

## WILLIAM ALLEN

*October* 21, 1885. When Allen was here the other day, I found that I could not take two steps with him. He taught school in Concord seventeen [?] years ago, and has not been here since. He wished much to see the town again, but nothing living and fair in it. He had, I should say, a very musty recollection of it. He called on no living creature among all his pupils, but insisted on going to the new burying-ground and reading all the epitaphs. I waited at the gate, telling him that that ground did not smell good. I remembered when the first body was placed in it. He did, however, ask after one or two juvenile scamps and one idiotic boy who came to school to him, — how they had turned out, — and also after a certain caged fool, dead since he was here, who had lived near where he boarded; also after a certain ancient tavern, now pulled down. This at odd intervals, for he improved all the rest of his time while he was here in attending a Sabbath-school convention.

### RICE'S SUCCESSFUL LIFE

*November* 17, 1855. It is interesting to me to talk with Rice,[1] he lives so thoroughly and satisfactorily to himself. He has learned that rare art of living, the very elements of which most professors do not know. His life has been not a failure but a success. Seeing me going to sharpen some plane-irons, and hearing me complain of the want of tools, he said that I ought to have a chest of tools. But I said it was not worth the while. I should not use them enough to pay for them. 'You would use them more, if you had them,' said he. 'When I came to do a piece of work I used to find commonly that I wanted a certain tool, and I made it a rule first always to make that tool. I have spent as much as $3000 thus on my tools.' Comparatively speaking, his life is a success; not such a failure as most men's. He gets more out of any enterprise than his neighbors, for he helps himself more and hires less. Whatever pleasure there is in it he enjoys. By good sense and calculation he has become rich and has invested his property well, yet practices a fair and neat economy, dwells not in untidy luxury. It costs him less to live, and he gets more out of life, than others. To get his living, or keep it, is not a hasty or disagreeable toil. He works slowly but surely, enjoying the sweet of it. He buys a piece of meadow at a profitable rate, works at it in pleasant weather, he and his son, when they are inclined, goes a-fishing or a-bee-hunting or a-rifle-shooting quite as often, and thus the meadow gets redeemed, and potatoes get planted, perchance, and he is very sure to have a good crop stored in his cellar in the fall, and some to sell. He always has the best of potatoes there. In the same spirit in

---

[1] Reuben Rice, who lived in the village.

which he and his son tackle up their Dobbin (he never keeps a fast horse) and go a-spearing or a-fishing through the ice, they also tackle up and go to their Sudbury farm to hoe or harvest a little, and when they return they bring home a load of stumps in their hay-rigging, which impeded their labors, but, perchance, supply them with their winter wood. All the woodchucks they shoot or trap in the bean-field are brought home also. And thus their life is a long sport and they know not what hard times are.

### MINOTT AND HIS CATS

*November* 19, 1855. Minott had two cats on his knee. One given away without his knowledge a fortnight before had just found its way back. He says he would not kill a cat for twenty dollars, — no, not for fifty. Finally he told his women folks that he would not do it for five hundred, or any sum. He thought they loved life as well as we. Johnny Vose wouldn't do it. He used to carry down milk to a shop every day for a litter of kittens.

### RICE'S TURTLE STORY

*November* 19, 1855. Rice told his turtle story the other night: 'One day I was going through Boston market and I saw a huddle of men around something or other. I edged my way between them and saw that they had got a great mud turtle on a plank, and a butcher stood over him with a cleaver in his hand. "Eh," said I, "what are you trying to do?" "We are waiting for him to put out his head so that we may cut it off. Look out," they said; "don't come so near, or he'll bite you." "Look here," said I, "let me try. I guess I can make him put his head out." "Let him try. Let him try," they said, with a laugh. So I stepped into the ring and stood astride of the turtle, while they looked on to see the sport. After looking at him a moment, I put down my hands and turned him over on to his back, whereupon he immediately ran out his head and pushed against the plank to turn himself back, but, as they were not ready to cut at once, or his neck was not in a good position, I seized his head in both hands and, putting my feet against his breast-bone, drew his head out the full length of his neck and said, "Now cut away. Only take care you don't cut my fingers." They cut, and I threw the head down on the floor. As I walked away, some one said, "I guess that fellow has seen mud turtles before to-day."'

BRINGING HOME THE BOAT

*November* 30, 1855. On the 27th, when I made my last voyage for the season, I found a large sound pine log about four feet long floating, and brought it home. Off the larger end I sawed two wheels, about a foot in diameter and seven or eight inches thick, and I fitted to them an axle-tree made of a joist, which also I found in the river, and thus I had a convenient pair of wheels on which to get my boat up and roll it about. The assessors called me into their office this year and said they wished to get an inventory of my property; asked if I had any real estate. No. Any notes at interest or railroad shares? No. Any taxable property? None that I knew of. 'I own a boat,' I said; and one of them thought that that might come under the head of a pleasure carriage, which is taxable. Now that I have wheels to it, it comes nearer to it. I was pleased to get my boat in by this means rather than on a borrowed wheelbarrow. It was fit that the river should furnish the material, and that in my last voyage on it, when the ice reminded me that it was time to put it in winter quarters.

## AN EQUITABLE DIVISION

*December* 29, 1855. When two men, Billings and Prichard, were dividing the stock of my father and Hurd,[1] the former acting for Father, P. was rather tight for Hurd. They came to a cracked bowl, at which P. hesitated and asked, 'Well, what shall we do with this?' B. took it in haste and broke it, and, presenting him one piece, said, 'There, that is your half and this is ours.'

## PICKEREL-FISHING

*January* 4, 1856. Aunt says that Mr. Hoar tells a story of Abel Davis to this purport: He had once caught a pickerel in the brook near his house and was overheard to say, 'Why, who'd 'a' thought to find you here in Temple Brook. With

[1] Isaac Hurd, with whom Thoreau's father conducted a dry-goods business in Concord for a short time.

a slice of pork you'll make Rhody' (or whatever the name of his wife was) 'and I a good meal.' He probably was not much of a fisherman, and could hardly contain himself for joy.

FAMILY REMINISCENCES

*January* 7, 1856.    Mother tried to milk the cow which Father took on trial, but she kicked at her and spilt the milk. (They say a dog had bitten her teats.)  Proctor laughed at her as a city girl, and then he tried, but the cow kicked him over, and he finished by beating her with his cowhide shoe. Captain Richardson milked her warily, standing up.  Father came home, and thought he would 'brustle right up to her,'

for she needed much to be milked, but suddenly she lifted her leg and 'struck him fair and square right in the muns,' knocked him flat, and broke the bridge of his nose, which shows it yet. He distinctly heard her hoof rattle on his nose. This 'started the claret,' and, without stanching the blood, he at once drove her home to the man he had her of. She ran at some young women by the way, who saved themselves by getting over the wall in haste.

Father complained of the powder in the meeting-house garret at town meeting, but it did not get moved while we lived there. Here he painted over his old signs for guide-boards, and got a fall when painting Hale's (?) factory. Here the bladder John was playing with burst on the hearth. The cow came into the entry after pumpkins. I cut my toe, and was knocked over by a hen with chickens, etc., etc.

Mother tells how, at the brick house, we each had a little garden a few feet square, and I came in one day, having found a potato just sprouted, which by her advice I planted in my garden. Ere long John came in with a potato which he had found and had it planted in his garden, — 'Oh, mother, I have found a potato all sprouted. I mean to put it in my garden,' etc. Even Helen is said to have found one. But next I came crying that somebody had got my potato, etc., etc., but it was restored to me as the youngest and original discoverer, if not inventor, of the potato, and it grew in *my* garden, and finally its crop was dug by myself and yielded a dinner for the family.

I was kicked down by a passing ox. Had a chicken given me by Lidy — Hannah — and peeped through the keyhole at it. Caught an eel with John. Went to bed with new boots on, and after with cap. 'Rasselas' given me, etc., etc. Asked P. Wheeler, 'Who owns all the land?' Asked Mother, having got the medal for geography, 'Is Boston in Concord?' If I had gone to Miss Wheeler a little longer, should have received the chief prize book, 'Henry Lord Mayor,' etc., etc.

### WALKING ON THE RIVER

*January* 26, 1856. Walked as far as Flint's Bridge with Abel Hunt, where I took to the river. I told him I had come to walk on the river as the best place, for the snow had drifted somewhat in the road, while it was converted into ice almost entirely on the river. 'But,' asked he, 'are you not afraid that you will get in?' 'Oh, no, it will bear a load of wood from one end to the other.' 'But then there may be some weak places.' Yet he is some seventy years old and was born and bred immediately on its banks. Truly one half the world does not know how the other half lives.

### MISS MARY EMERSON

*January* 26, 1856. Talking with Miss Mary Emerson this evening, she said, 'It was not the fashion to be so original when I was young.' She is readier to take my view — look through my eyes for the time — than any young person that I know in the town.

## A TALK WITH THE FISHERMEN

*February* 8, 1856. Edward and Isaac Garfield were fishing there, and Puffer came along, and afterward Lewis Miner with his gun. He cannot get near the partridges on account of the cracklings of the crust. I saw the last two approaching with my glass.

The fishermen agree in saying that the pickerel have generally been eating, and are full, when they bite. Puffer thinks they eat a good deal, but seldom. Some think it best to cut the holes the day before, because the noise frightens them; and the crackling of the crust to-day was thought to frighten them. E. Garfield says that his Uncle Daniel was once scaling a pickerel, where he pricked his finger against the horn of a pout which the pickerel had swallowed. He himself killed a pickerel with a paddle, in the act of swallowing a large perch. Puffer had taken a striped snake out of one.

They send to Lowell for their bait, and fishermen send thither from far and wide, so that there is not a sufficient supply for them. I. Garfield once caught an eel there with his pickerel bait, through the ice; also speared a trout that weighed three and a half pounds, he says, off Well Meadow.

E. Garfield says that he was just turning into the pond from up-stream when he heard a loud sound and saw and caught those two great mud turtles. He let the boat drift down upon them. One had got the other by the neck, and their shells were thumping together and their tails sticking up. He caught one in each hand suddenly, and succeeded in getting them into the boat only by turning them over, since they resisted with their claws against the side; then stood on them turned over, paddled to nearest shore, pulled his boat up with his heel, and, taking a tail in each hand, walked backward through the meadow in water a foot deep, dragging them; then carried one a few rods, left him and returned for the other, and so on. One weighed forty-three and the other forty-seven pounds, together ninety. Puffer said that he never saw two together so heavy. I. Garfield said that he had seen one that weighed sixty-three pounds. All referred to the time when (about fifteen years ago; one said the year of the Bunker Hill Monument celebration) some forty were found dead on the meadows between there and Sudbury. It was about the end of March, and Puffer inferred that they had come out thus early from the river, and, the water going down, the ice had settled on them and killed them; but the Garfields thought that the ice, which tore up the meadows very much that year, exposed them and so they froze. I think the last most likely. Puffer searches for them in May under the cranberry vines with a spear, and calls one of the small kinds the 'grass tortoise.'

E. Garfield says that he saw the other day where a fox had caught in the snow three partridges and eaten two. He himself last winter caught two, on the hillside south of Fair Haven, with his hands. They flew before him and dived into the snow, which was about a foot deep, going twice their length into it. He thrust his hand in and caught them. Puffer said that his companion one night speared a partridge on the alders on the south side the pond.

E. Garfield says there were many quails here last fall, but that they are suffering now. One night as he was spearing on Conant's cranberry meadow, just north the pond, his dog caught a sheldrake in the water by the shore. Some days ago he saw what he thought a hawk, as white as snow, fly over the pond, but it *may* have been a white owl (which last he never saw). He sometimes sees a hen-hawk in the winter, but never a partridge or other small hawk at this season. Speaks again of that large speckled hawk he killed once,

# PLATE VIII

*Fishing Through the Ice*

which some called a 'Cape eagle.' Had a hum-bird's nest behind their house last summer, and was amused to see the bird drive off other birds; would pursue a robin and alight on his back; let none come near. I. Garfield saw one's nest on a horizontal branch of a white pine near the Charles Miles house, about seven feet from ground. E. Garfield spoke of the wren's nest as not uncommon, hung in the grass of the meadows, and how swiftly and easily the bird would run through a winrow of hay.

Puffer saw a couple of foxes cross the pond a few days ago. The wheelwright in the Corner saw four at once, about the same time.

### POPULAR ASTRONOMY

*February* 10, 1856. Speaking about the weather and the fishing with E. and I. Garfield on the 8th, I was amused to hear these two young farmers suddenly disputing as to whether the moon (?), if that be it, was in the Feet or the Head or elsewhere. Though I know far more of astronomy than they, I should not know how at once to find out this nonsense in an almanac. Yet they talk very glibly about it, and go a-fishing accordingly. Again, in the evening of the same day, I overtook Mr. Prichard and observed that it was time for a thaw, but said he, 'That does not look like it,' pointing to the moon in the west. 'You could hang a powder-horn upon that pretty well.'

## A CALL AT MILES'S SAWMILL

*February* 28, 1856.  Miles [1] is repairing the damage done at his new mill by the dam giving way. He is shovelling out the flume, which was half filled with sand, standing in the water. His sawmill, built of slabs, reminds me of a new country. He has lost a head of water equal to two feet by this accident. Yet he sets his mill agoing to show me how it works. What a smell as of gun-wash when he raised the gate! He calls it the sulphur from the pond. It must be the carburetted hydrogen gas from the bottom of the pond under the ice. It powerfully scents the whole mill. A powerful smelling-bottle. How pleasant are the surroundings of a mill! Here are the logs (pail-stuff), already drawn to the door from a neighboring hill before the mill is in operation. The dammed-up meadow, the meadow [*sic*], the melted snow, and welling springs are the serf he compels to do his work. He is unruly as yet, has lately broken loose, filled up the flume, and flooded the fields below. He uses the dam of an old mill which stood here a hundred years ago, which now nobody knows anything about. The mill is built of slabs, of the worm-eaten sap-wood. The old dam had probably been undermined by muskrats. It would have been most prudent to have built a new one. Rude forces, rude men, and rude appliances.

Martial Miles, who is there, says that there are many trout in this brook. He sees them running down just before winter, and at that time Charles Snow once speared a great many, one weighing four pounds. He once came within four feet of an otter at 10 P. M., in the middle of the road, by the guide-board just north of this brook. Spoke of the one

[1] Warren Miles, who had a sawmill on Nut Meadow Brook.

shot in a ditch at Donge Hole, as I had heard before; also of
the three killed (shot) at Farrar's Swamp. The one who shot
them told him that he attempted to kill them with a shovel,
but that they would take it out of his hands as often as he
attempted it.

### THE HUNTER AND HIS EYES

*February* 28, 1856. Coombs came along with his dog and
gun, on his way to shoot partridges, which will come out to
bud this evening on certain young apple trees. He has got
four or five for several nights in succession, and sees foxes
there, running about on the crust. Francis Wheeler says he
sold two young fox-skins to a tin peddler to-day for a dollar.
Coombs says they got a silver-gray fox in Lincoln this winter,
and sold its skin for sixteen dollars! He says that he killed a
sheldrake a month or six weeks ago in a small open place beneath the falls at the factory. This shows what hardy birds
they are. Last summer he found a black duck's nest on one
of the islands in Loring's Pond. He saw the duck hide in the
grass, came up, and put his hand on a parcel of feathers and,
raising a handful, was surprised to find the eggs under them.

How various are the talents of men! From the brook in
which one lover of nature has never during all his lifetime
detected anything larger than a minnow, another extracts
a trout that weighs three pounds, or an otter four feet long.
How much more game he will see who carries a gun, *i. e.* who
goes to see it! Though you roam the woods all your days,
you never will see by chance what he sees who goes on purpose to see it. One gets his living by shooting woodcocks;
most never see one in their lives.

Coombs goes to shoot partridges this evening by a far-off wood-side, and M. Miles goes home to load up, for he is going to Boston with a load of wood to-night.

## MINOTT AND EMERSON

*February* 29, 1856. Minott told me this afternoon of his catching a pickerel in the Mill Brook once, — before the pond was drawn off, when the brook had four or five times as much water as now, — which weighed four pounds. Says they stayed in it all winter in those days. This was near his land up the brook. He once also caught there, when fishing for pickerel, a trout which weighed three and a half pounds. He fell within two feet of the water, but he succeeded in tossing him higher up. When cutting peat thereabouts, he saw a stinkpot turtle in the water eating a frog which it had just caught. Speaks of seeing a mink swimming along a little run in his beech wood-lot, and from time to time running along the shore; part way up an alder and down again.

He loves to recall his hunting days and adventures, and I willingly listen to the stories he has told me half a dozen times already. One day he saw about twenty black ducks on Goose Pond, and stole down on them, thinking to get a shot, but it chanced that a stray dog scared them up before he was ready. He stood on the point of the neck of land between the ponds, and watched them as they flew high toward Flint's Pond. As he looked, he saw one separate from the flock when they had got half-way to Flint's Pond, or half a mile, and return straight toward Goose Pond again. He thought he would await him, and give him a shot if he came near enough. As he flew pretty near and rather low, he fired, whereupon the duck rose right up high into the air, and he saw by his motions that he was wounded. Suddenly he dropped, by a slanting fall, into the point of a thick pine wood, and he heard him plainly strike the ground like a stone. He went there and searched for a long time, and was about giving it up, when at length he saw the duck standing, still alive and bleeding, by the side of a stump, and made out to kill him with a stick before he could reach the water.

He said he saw Emerson come home from lecturing the other day with his knitting-bag (lecture-bag) in his hand. He asked him if the lecturing business was as good as it used to be. Emerson said he didn't see but it was as good as ever; guessed the people would want lectures 'as long as he or I lived.'

Told again of the partridge hawk striking down a partridge which rose before him and flew across the run in the beech woods, — how suddenly he did it, — and he, hearing the fluttering of the partridge, came up and secured it, while the hawk kept out of gun-shot.

### HAYNES'S AXE-HELVES

*March* 1, 1856. Haynes of Sudbury brought some axe-helves which he had been making to Smith's shop to sell to-day. Those made by hand are considered stronger than those which are turned, because their outline conforms to the grain. They told him they had not sold any of the last yet. 'Well,' said he, 'you may depend on it you will. They've got to come after them yet, for they haven't been able to get into the woods this winter on account of the snow, and they'll have to do all their chopping this month.'

I like to see the farmer whittling his own axe-helve, as I did E. Hosmer a white oak one on the 27th *ult.*

### TWO FRIENDS

*March 4, 1856.* I had two friends. The one offered me friendship on such terms that I could not accept it, without a sense of degradation. He would not meet me on equal terms, but only be to some extent my patron. He would not come to see me, but was hurt if I did not visit him. He would not readily accept a favor, but would gladly confer one. He treated me with ceremony occasionally, though he could be simple and downright sometimes; and from time to time acted a part, treating me as if I were a distinguished stranger; was on stilts, using made words. Our relation was one long tragedy, yet I did not directly speak of it. I do not believe in complaint, nor in explanation. The whole is but too plain, alas, already. We grieve that we do not love each other, that we cannot confide in each other. I could not bring myself to speak, and so recognize an obstacle to our affection.

I had another friend, who, through a slight obtuseness, perchance, did not recognize a fact which the dignity of friendship would by no means allow me to descend so far as to speak of, and yet the inevitable effect of that ignorance was to hold us apart forever.

## WHAT BEFELL AT MRS. BROOKS'S [1]

*March* 19, 1856.   On the morning of the 17th, Mrs. Brooks's Irish girl Joan fell down the cellar stairs, and was found by her mistress lying at the bottom, apparently lifeless. Mrs. Brooks ran to the street-door for aid to get her up, and asked a Miss Farmer, who was passing, to call the blacksmith near by. The latter lady turned instantly, and, making haste across the road on this errand, fell flat in a puddle of melted snow, and came back to Mrs. Brooks's, bruised and dripping and asking for opodeldoc. Mrs. Brooks again ran to the door and called to George Bigelow to complete the unfinished errand. He ran nimbly about it and fell flat in another puddle near the former, but, his joints being limber, got along without opodeldoc and raised the blacksmith. He also notified James Burke, who was passing, and he, rushing in to render aid, fell off one side of the cellar stairs in the dark. They no sooner got the girl up-stairs than she came to and went raving, then had a fit.

Haste makes waste. It never rains but it pours. I have this from those who had heard Mrs. Brooks's story, seen the girl, the stairs, and the puddles.


## STORIES OF UNCLE CHARLES

*April* 3, 1856.   People are talking about my Uncle Charles. Minott tells how he heard Tilly Brown once asking him to show him a peculiar (inside?) lock in wrestling. 'Now, don't

[1] Thoreau's own title.

hurt me, don't throw me hard.' He struck his antagonist inside his knees with his feet, and so deprived him of his legs. Hosmer remembers his tricks in the barroom, shuffling cards, etc. He could do anything with cards, yet he did not gamble. He would toss up his hat, twirling it over and over, and catch it on his head invariably. Once wanted to live at Hosmer's, but the latter was afraid of him. 'Can't we study up something?' he asked. H. asked him into the house and brought out apples and cider, and Charles talked. 'You!' said he, 'I burst the bully of Lowell' (or Haverhill?). He wanted to wrestle; would not be put off. 'Well, we won't wrestle in the house.' So they went out to the yard, and a crowd got round. 'Come spread some straw here,' said C. 'I don't want to hurt him.' He threw him at once. They tried again. He told them to spread more straw and he 'burst' him.

He had a strong head and never got drunk; would drink gin sometimes, but not to excess. Did not use tobacco, except snuff out of another's box sometimes. Was very neat in his person. Was not profane, though vulgar. . . .

Uncle Charles used to say that he hadn't a single tooth in his head. The fact was they were all double, and I have heard that he lost about all of them by the time he was twenty-one. Ever since I knew him he could swallow his nose.

### LIMITED KNOWLEDGE

*April 3,* 1856. Very few men take a wide survey; their knowledge is very limited and particular. I talked with an old man the other day about the snow, hoping he would give me some information about past winters. I said, 'I guess you don't remember so much old snow on the ground at this

season.' He answered, 'I never saw the snow so deep between my house and John's.' It wasn't a stone's throw.[1]

### JOHN GOODWIN MUSKRAT-SHOOTING

*April* 8, 1856. Hear the crack of Goodwin's piece close by,
just as I reach my boat. He has killed another rat. Asks if
I am bound up-stream. 'Yes, to Well Meadow.' Says I
can't get above the hay-path a quarter of a mile above on
account of ice; if he could, he'd 'a' been at Well Meadow
before now. But I think I will try, and he thinks if I succeed he will try it. By standing on oars, which sink several

[1] The same man in summer of '59 said he never saw the river so low!! Of
what use to be old? [Thoreau's pencil note.]

inches, and hauling over one cake of ice, I manage to break my way into an open canal above, where I soon see three rats swimming. Goodwin says that he got twenty-four minks last winter, more than ever before in one season; trapped most, shot only two or three.

## DEACON TARBELL

*April* 28, 1856. How promising a simple, unpretending, quiet, somewhat reserved man, whether among generals or scholars or farmers! How rare an equanimity and serenity which are an encouragement to all observers! Some youthfulness, some manliness, some goodness. Like Tarbell, a man apparently made a deacon on account of some goodness, and not on account of some hypocrisy and badness as usual.

## 'PERCH' HOSMER

*June* 4, 1856. Anthony Wright says that he used to get slippery elm bark from a place southwest of Wetherbee's Mill, about ten rods south of the brook. He says there was once a house at head of hollow next beyond Clamshell. Pointed out the site of 'Perch' Hosmer's house in the small field south of road this side of Cozzens's; all smooth now. Dr. Heywood worked over him a fortnight, while the perch was dissolving in his throat. He got little compassion generally, and the nickname 'Perch' into the bargain. Think of going to sleep for fourteen nights with a perch, his fins set

and his scales (!), dissolving in your throat!! What dreams!
What waking thoughts!

## A WEATHER COCK

*July* 25, 1856.  The haymakers getting in the hay from
Hubbard's meadow tell me the cock says we are going to
have a long spell of dry weather or else very wet. 'Well,
there's some difference between them,' I answer; 'how do
you know it?' 'I just heard a cock crow at noon, and that's
a sure sign it will either be very dry or very wet.'

## CATCHING A PIG

*August* 8, 1856.  3.30 P. M. — When I came forth, thinking to
empty my boat and go a-meditating along the river, — for
the full ditches and drenched grass forbade other routes,
except the highway, — and this is one advantage of a boat,
— I learned to my chagrin that Father's pig was gone. He
had leaped out of the pen some time since his breakfast, but
his dinner was untouched. Here was an ugly duty not to be
shirked, — a wild shoat that weighed but ninety to be
tracked, caught, and penned, — an afternoon's work, at
least (if I were lucky enough to accomplish it so soon), prepared for me, quite different from what I had anticipated.
I felt chagrined, it is true, but I could not ignore the fact
nor shirk the duty that lay so near to me. Do the duty that
lies nearest to thee. I proposed to Father to sell the pig as

he was running (somewhere) to a neighbor who had talked
of buying him, making a considerable reduction.  But my
suggestion was not acted on, and the responsibilities of the
case all devolved on me, for I could run faster than Father.
Father looked to me, and I ceased to look to the river.  Well,
let us see if we can track him.  Yes, this is the corner where
he got out, making a step of his trough.  Thanks to the rain,
his tracks are quite distinct.  Here he went along the edge
of the garden over the water- and musk-melons, then through
the beans and potatoes, and even along the front-yard walk
I detect the print of his divided hoof, his two sharp toes
(*ungulæ*).  It's a wonder we did not see him.  And here he
passed out under the gate, across the road, — how naked he
must have felt! — into a grassy ditch, and whither next?  Is
it of any use to go hunting him up unless you have devised
some mode of catching him when you have found?  Of what
avail to know where he has been, even where he is?  He was
so shy the little while we had him, of course he will never
come back; he cannot be tempted by a swill-pail.  Who
knows how many miles off he is!  Perhaps he has taken the
back track and gone to Brighton, or Ohio!  At most, probably we shall only have the satisfaction of glimpsing the
nimble beast at a distance, from time to time, as he trots
swiftly through the green meadows and corn-fields.  But,
now I speak, what is that I see pacing deliberately up the
middle of the street forty rods off?  It is *he*.  As if to tantalize,
to tempt us to waste our afternoon without further hesitation, he thus offers himself.  He roots a foot or two and then
lies down on his belly in the middle of the street.  But think
not to catch him a-napping.  He has his eyes about, and his
ears too.  He has already been chased.  He gives that wagon
a wide berth, and now, seeing me, he turns and trots back
down the street.  He turns into a front yard.  Now if I can
only close that gate upon him ninety-nine hundredths of

the work is done, but ah! he hears me coming afar off, he foresees the danger, and, with swinish cunning and speed, he scampers out. My neighbor in the street tries to head him; he jumps to this side the road, then to that, before him; but the third time the pig was there first and went by. 'Whose is it?' he shouts. 'It's ours.' He bolts into that neighbor's yard and so across his premises. He has been twice there before, it seems; he knows the road; see what work he has made in his flower-garden! He must be fond of bulbs. Our neighbor picks up one tall flower with its bulb attached, holds it out at arm's length. He is excited about the pig; it is a subject he is interested in. But where is he gone now? The last glimpse I had of him was as he went through the cow-yard; here are his tracks again in this corn-field, but they are lost in the grass. We lose him; we beat the bushes in vain; he may be far away. But hark! I heard a grunt. Nevertheless for half an hour I do not see him that grunted. At last I find fresh tracks along the river, and again lose them. Each neighbor whose garden I traverse tells me some anecdote of losing pigs, or the attempt to drive them, by which I am not encouraged. Once more he crosses our first neighbor's garden and is said to be in the road. But I am not there yet; it is a good way off. At length my eyes rest on him again, after three quarters of an hour's separation. There he trots with the whole road to himself, and now again drops on his belly in a puddle. Now he starts again, seeing me twenty rods off, deliberates, considers which way I want him to go, and goes the other. There was some chance of driving him along the sidewalk, or letting him go rather, till he slipped under our gate again, but of what avail would that be? How corner and catch him who keeps twenty rods off? He never lets the open side of the triangle be less than half a dozen rods wide. There was one place where a nar-rower street turned off at right angles with the main one, just this side our yard, but I could not drive him past that. Twice he ran up the narrow street, for he knew I did not wish it, but though the main street was broad and open and no traveller in sight, when I tried to drive him past this opening he invariably turned his piggish head toward me, dodged from side to side, and finally ran up the narrow street or down the main one, as if there were a high barrier erected before him. But really he is no more obstinate than I. I cannot but respect his tactics and his independence. He will be he, and I may be I. He is not unreasonable because he thwarts me, but only the more reasonable. He has a strong will. He stands upon his idea. There is a wall across the path not where a man bars the way, but where he is resolved not to travel. Is he not superior to man therein? Once more he glides down the narrow street, deliberates at a corner, chooses wisely for him, and disappears through an openwork fence eastward. He has gone to fresh gardens and pastures new. Other neighbors stand in the doorways but half sympathizing, only observing, 'Ugly thing to catch.' 'You have a job on your hands.' I lose sight of him, but hear that he is far ahead in a large field. And there we try to let him alone a while, giving him a wide berth.

At this stage an Irishman was engaged to assist. 'I can catch him,' says he, with Buonapartean confidence. He thinks him a family Irish pig. His wife is with him, bareheaded, and his little flibbertigibbet of a boy, seven years old. 'Here, Johnny, do you run right off there' (at the broadest possible angle with his own course). 'Oh, but he can't do anything,' 'Oh, but I only want him to tell me where he is, — to keep sight of him.' Michael soon discovers that he is not an Irish pig, and his wife and Johnny's occupation are soon gone. Ten minutes afterward I am patiently tracking him step by step through a corn-field, a near-sighted man helping me, and then into garden after garden

far eastward, and finally into the highway, at the graveyard; but hear and see nothing. One suggests a dog to track
him. Father is meanwhile selling him to the blacksmith, who
also is trying to get sight of him. After fifteen minutes
since he disappeared eastward, I hear that he has been to the
river twice far on [?] the north, through the first neighbor's
premises. I wend that way. He crosses the street far ahead,
Michael behind; he dodges up an avenue. I stand in the
gap there, Michael at the other end, and now he tries to
corner him. But it is a vain hope to corner him in a yard. I
see a carriage-manufactory door open. 'Let him go in there,
Flannery.' For once the pig and I are of one mind; he bolts
in, and the door is closed. Now for a rope. It is a large barn,
crowded with carriages. The rope is at length obtained; the
windows are barred with carriages lest he bolt through. He
is resting quietly on his belly in the further corner, thinking
unutterable things.

Now the course recommences within narrower limits.
Bump, bump, bump he goes, against wheels and shafts.
We get no hold yet. He is all ear and eye. Small boys are
sent under the carriages to drive him out. He froths at the
mouth and deters them. At length he is stuck for an instant
between the spokes of a wheel, and I am securely attached
to his hind leg. He squeals deafeningly, and is silent. The
rope is attached to a hind leg. The door is opened, and the
*driving* commences. Roll an egg as well. You may drag him,
but you cannot drive him. But he is in the road, and now
another thunder-shower greets us. I leave Michael with the
rope in one hand and a switch in the other and go home. He
seems to be gaining a little westward. But, after long delay,
I look out and find that he makes but doubtful progress. A
boy is made to face him with a stick, and it is only when the
pig springs at him savagely that progress is made homeward.
He will be killed before he is driven home. I get a wheel-

barrow and go to the rescue. Michael is alarmed. The pig is rabid, snaps at him. We drag him across the barrow, hold him down, and so, at last, get him home.

If a wild shoat like this gets loose, first track him if you can, or otherwise discover where he is. Do not scare him more than you can help. Think of some yard or building or other inclosure that will hold him and, by showing your forces — yet as if uninterested parties — fifteen or twenty rods off, let him of his own accord enter it. Then slightly shut the gate. Now corner and tie him and put him into a cart or barrow.

All progress in driving at last was made by facing and endeavoring to switch him from home. He rushed upon you and made a few feet in the desired direction. When I approached with the barrow he advanced to meet it with determination.

So I get home at dark, wet through and supperless, covered with mud and wheel-grease, without any rare flowers.

### ANOTHER PIG-CHASE

*August* 26, 1856. Last Friday (the 22d) afternoon (when I was away), Father's pig got out again and took to the riverside. The next day he was heard from, but not found. That night he was seen on an island in the meadow, in the midst of the flood, but thereafter for some time no account of him. J. Farmer advised to go to Ai Hale, just over the Carlisle line. He has got a dog which, if you put him on the track of the pig not more than four hours old, will pursue and catch him and hold him by the ear without hurting him till you come up. That's the best way. Ten men cannot stop him

in the road, but he will go by them. It was generally conceded that the right kind of dog was all that was wanted,
like Ai Hale's, one that would hold him by the ear, but not
uselessly maim him. One or two said, 'If I only had such a
one's dog, I'd catch him for so much.'

Neighbors sympathized as much as in them lay. It was
the town talk; the meetings were held at Wolcott & Holden's.
Every man told of his losses and disappointments in this line.
One had heard of his pig last up in Westford, but never saw
him again; another had only caught his pig by his running
against a post so hard as to stun himself for a few moments.
It was thought this one must have been born in the woods,
for he would run and leap like a wolf. Some advised not
to build so very high, but lay the upper board flat over the
pen, for then, when he caught by his fore feet, his body
would swing under to no purpose. One said you would not
catch him to buy a pig out of a drove. Our pig ran as if he
*still* had the devil in him. It was generally conceded that a
good dog was the desideratum. But thereupon Lawrence,
the harness-maker, came forward and told his experience.
He once helped hunt a pig in the next town. He weighed two
hundred; had been out some time (though not in '75), but
they learned where he resorted; but they got a capital dog of
the right kind. They had the dog tied lest he should scare the
pig too soon. They crawled along very carefully near to the
hollow where the pig was till they could hear him. They
knew that if he should hear them and he was wide awake, he
would dash off with a grunt, and that would be the last of
him, but what more could they do? They consulted in a
whisper and concluded to let the dog go. They did so, and
directly heard an awful yelp; rushed up; the pig was gone,
and there lay the dog torn all to pieces! At this there was a
universal *haw! haw!* and the reputation of dogs fell, and the
chance of catching the pig seemed less.

Two dollars reward was offered to him who would catch and return him without maiming him. At length, the 26th, he was heard from. He was caught and tied in north part of the town. Took to a swamp, as they say they are inclined. He was chased two hours with a spaniel dog, which never faced him, nor touched him, but, as the man said, 'tuckered him out,' kept him on the go and showed where he was. When at a distance the pig stopped and faced the dog until the pursuers came up. He was brought home the 27th, all his legs tied, and put into his new pen. It was a very deep one. It might have been made deeper, but Father did not wish to build a wall, and the man who caught him and got his two dollars for it thought it ought to hold any decent pig. Father said he didn't wish to keep him in a well.

### CIVIC DUTIES AND LITERATURE

*September* 2, 1856. My father asked John Legross if he took an interest in politics and did his duty to his country at this crisis. He said he did. He went into the wood-shed and read the newspaper Sundays. Such is the dawn of the literary taste, the first seed of literature that is planted in the new country. His grandson may be the author of a Bhagvat-Geeta.

## CONCORD, THE SACRED RIVER

*September* 2, 1856. There was an old gentleman here to-day who lived in Concord when he was young and remembers how Dr. Ripley [1] talked to him and other little boys from the pulpit, as they came into church with their hands full of lilies, saying that those lilies looked so fresh that they must have been gathered that morning! Therefore they must have committed the sin of bathing this morning! Why, this is as sacred a river as the Ganges, sir.

## MORE OF MINOTT'S STORIES

*September* 30, 1856. Minott tells of a General Hull,[2] who lived somewhere in this county, who, he remembers, called out the whole division once or twice to a muster. He sold the army under him to the English in the last war, — though General Miller of Lincoln besought him to let him lead them, — and never was happy after it, had no peace of mind. It was said that his life was in danger here in consequence of his treason. Once, at a muster in front of the Hayden house, when there was a sham fight, and an Indian party took a circuit round a piece of wood, some put green grapes into their guns, and he, hearing one whistle by his head, thought some one wished to shoot him and ordered them to disperse, — dismissed them.

[1] Rev. Ezra Ripley, D.D. (1751–1841), the Concord minister, who lived in the 'Old Manse' before Hawthorne.

[2] Gen. William Hull, whose home was in Newton, Massachusetts.

Speaking of the meadow-hay which is lost this year, Minott said that the little they had got since the last flood before this was good for nothing, would only poison the cattle, being covered with the dried slime and filth of the freshet. When you mowed it there arose a great dust. He spoke of this grass, thus left over winter to next year, as 'old fog.' Said that Clark (Daniel or Brooks) asked him the other day what made so many young alders and birches and willows spring up in the river meadows of late years; it didn't use to be so forty or fifty years ago; and he told him that in old times, when they were accustomed to take something strong to drink, they didn't stand for such shrubs but mowed all clear as they went, but now, not feeling so much energy for want of the stimulant, when they came to a bush, though no bigger than a pipe-stem, they mowed all round it and left it standing.

### FOUR BOYS AND A HORSE

*October* 2, 1856. I am amused to see four little Irish boys only five or six years old getting a horse in a pasture, for their father apparently, who is at work in a neighboring field. They have all in a row got hold of a very long halter and are leading him. All wish to have a hand in it. It is surprising that he obeys such small specimens of humanity, but he seems to be very docile, a real family horse. At length, by dint of pulling and shouting, they get him into a run down a hill, and though he moves very deliberately, scarcely faster than a walk, all but the one at the end of the line soon cut and run to right and left, without having looked behind, expecting him to be upon them. They haul up at last at the bars, which are down, and then the family puppy, a brown

pointer (?), about two-thirds grown, comes bounding to join them and assist. He is as youthful and about as knowing as any of them. The horse marches gravely behind, obeying the faint tug at the halter, or honestly stands still from time to time, as if not aware that they are pulling at all, though they are all together straining every nerve to start him. It is interesting to behold this faithful beast, the oldest and wisest of the company, thus implicitly obeying the lead of the youngest and weakest.

### AN OLD CONCORD SHOPKEEPER

*October* 11, 1856. E. Hosmer said yesterday that his father remembered when there was but one store in Concord, and that the little office attached to Dr. Heywood's house, kept by Beatton.... Perhaps, then, Jones was the only shop-

keeper in *his* day. I was speaking of it to Farrar, the blacksmith, to-day, and he said, yes, he had heard his father
speak of Beatton as 'the most honestest man that ever was.'
When a child was sent to his store and he could not make
change within half a penny he would stick a row of pins in
the child's sleeve, enough to make all square. He said he had
only a keg of molasses and a bladder of snuff when he began.
Farrar thought that the spirit manufactured a century ago
was not so adulterated and poisonous as that now made.
He could remember when delirium tremens was very rare.
There was Luke Dodge; he could remember him a drunkard
for more than forty years, yet he was now between eighty
and ninety.

### ONE OF MINOTT'S HUNTING STORIES

*October* 18, 1856. Minott told me one of his hunting stories
yesterday, how he saw a very large hen-hawk come sailing
from over the hill, just this side of where Moore lives now.
He didn't expect to reach her, but he knew that he had a
plaguy smart little piece, — it was a kind of half-stocked one
(he always speaks of the gun he used on a particular occasion
as if it were a new one, describing it minutely, though he
never had more than three, perhaps not more than two, in
his life, I suspect), — so he thought he'd give her a try, and,
faith, she pitched down into the little meadow on the north
side the road there, and when he came up she bristled up to
him so that he was obliged to give her another charge.

## ANOTHER CHAT WITH MINOTT

*October* 21, 1856. Had a chat with Minott, sitting on a log by his door. He says he began to carry a gun when he was fifteen or sixteen years old; afterward he owned three at one time, one training-piece and two fowling-pieces. He lived at James Baker's seven years; not till after he was of age. He used to range all over that neighborhood, away down into Lexington, and knew every stone and stump; used to go chestnutting about Flint's Pond, and a-fishing there, too. The fish and fowl were ten times as plenty as they are now. Why, he has been along the ridges (the moraines toward Ditch Pond) when, the ducks rising up on each side, the sky was black with them. His training-piece was an old king's-arm, taken from the British some time, he supposed. It was a capital piece, even for shot, and thoroughly made, made upon honor every part of it. There are no such guns made in this country. The lock was strong and smart, so that when you snapped it, it filled the pan chock-full of fire, and he could burn a single kernel of powder in it. But it took a good deal of powder to load it. He kept its brass mountings burnished so bright that you could see your face in them. He had also owned a French piece. Once, too, he had a little English cocking-piece, *i. e.* fowling-piece. It had the word 'London' on the barrel close to the lock. It was a plaguy smart piece, bell-muzzled, and would carry ball well. He could knock over a robin with it eight rods off with ball or a slug. He had a rifle once. What did they use rifles for? Oh, for turkey-shooting.

Once, one Rice, who lived in Lincoln where Hayden does now, made a turkey-shooting, and he went to it with his English fowling-piece. He saw many on the road going to it. Saw Dakin and Jonas Minott (Captain Minott's son, who spent quite a fortune on shooting), one offering to take another down to the shooting for a mug of flip. They asked him what he was going to do with that little thing. You paid fourpence a shot at a live turkey only twenty rods off. Those who had rifles were not allowed to rest. Amos Baker was there (who was at Concord Fight). The turkey was a large white one. Minott rammed down his slug and, getting down behind a fence, rested on it while the rest laughed at him. He told Amos to look sharp and tell him where his ball struck, and fired. Amos said the ball struck just above the turkey. Others were firing in the meanwhile. Minott loaded and tried once more, and this time his ball cut off the turkey's neck, and it was his; worth a dollar, at least. You only had to draw blood to get the turkey. Another, a black one, was set up, and this time his ball struck the ground just this side the turkey, then scaled up and passed right through its body, lodging under the skin on the opposite side, and he cut it out.

Rice made his money chiefly by his liquor, etc. Some set up the turkeys they had gained: others 'hustled' for liquor or for a supper; i. e., they would take sides and then, putting seven coppers in a hat, shake them up well and empty them, and the party that got the fewest heads after three casts paid for the supper.

M. says that, in all the time he lived at Baker's, in fact in all his life, he never went to market.

Told me how they used to carry on, on Concord Common formerly, on great days. Once, when they were shaking dice there in the evening for money, round a table with twenty-five or thirty dollars in cash upon it, some rogue fastened a rope to one leg of the table, and so at a distance suddenly started off with the table, at the same time upsetting and extinguishing the light. This made a great outcry. They ran

up crying, 'Mister, I'll help you pick up your money,' but
they put the half into their own pockets.

## A HUNGRY YANKEE

*November* 30, 1856.   Minott told me on Friday of an oldish
man and woman who had brought to a muster here once a
great leg of bacon boiled, to turn a penny with. The skin,
as thick as sole-leather, was flayed and turned back, dis-
playing the tempting flesh. A tall, raw-boned, omnivorous
heron of a Yankee came along and bargained with the
woman, who was awaiting a customer, for as much of that as
he could eat. He ate and ate and ate, making a surprising
hole, greatly to the amusement of the lookers-on, till the
woman in her despair, unfaithful to her engagement, ap-
pealed to the police to drive him off.

## A NEW ENGLAND FARMER

*December* 1, 1856.   I see the old pale-faced farmer out again
on his sled now for the five-thousandth time, — Cyrus Hubbard, a man of a certain New England probity and worth,
immortal and natural, like a natural product, like the sweet-
ness of a nut, like the toughness of hickory. He, too, is a
redeemer for me. How superior actually to the faith he
professes! He is not an office-seeker. What an institution,
what a revelation is a man! We are wont foolishly to think
that the creed which a man professes is more significant than

the fact he is. It matters not how hard the conditions seemed, how mean the world, for a man is a prevalent force and a new law himself. He is a system whose law is to be observed. The old farmer condescends to countenance still this nature and order of things. It is a great encouragement that an honest man makes this world his abode. He rides on the sled drawn by oxen, world-wise, yet comparatively so young, as if they had seen scores of winters. The farmer spoke to me, I can swear, clean, cold, moderate as the snow. He does not melt the snow where he treads. Yet what a faint impression that encounter may make on me after all! Moderate, natural, true, as if he were made of earth, stone, wood, snow. I thus meet in this universe kindred of mine, composed of these elements. I see men like frogs; their peeping I partially understand.

### GRATITUDE FOR MELVIN

*December* 2, 1856. Saw Melvin's lank bluish-white black-spotted hound, and Melvin [1] with his gun near, going home at eve. He follows hunting, praise be to him, as regularly in our tame fields as the farmers follow farming. Persistent Genius! How I respect him and thank him for him! [*sic*] I trust the Lord will provide us with another Melvin when he is gone. How good in him to follow his own bent, and not continue at the Sabbath-school all his days! What a wealth he thus becomes in the neighborhood! Few know how to take the census. I thank my stars for Melvin. I think of him with gratitude when I am going to sleep, grateful that he exists, — that Melvin who is such a trial to his

[1] George Melvin, who lived on the Lowell road.

mother. Yet he is agreeable to me as a tinge of russet on the
hillside. I would fain give thanks morning and evening for
my blessings. Awkward, gawky, loose-hung, dragging his
legs after him. He is my contemporary and neighbor. He
is one tribe, I am another, and we are not at war.

### IMPROVING THE FIRST SNOW

*December* 2, 1856. How quickly men come out on to the
highways with their sleds and improve the first snow! The
farmer has begun to play with his sled as early as any of the
boys. See him already with mittens on and thick boots well
greased — been soaking in grease all summer, perhaps —
and fur cap and red comforter about his throat, though
it is not yet cold, walking beside his team with contented
thoughts. This drama every day in the streets! This is the
theatre I go to. There he goes with his venture behind him,
and often he gets aboard for a change.

### BRAVE WORDS

*December* 3, 1856. A man killed at the fatal Lincoln Bridge
died in the village the other night. The only words he uttered
while he lingered in his delirium were 'All right,' probably
the last which he had uttered before he was struck, — brave,
prophetic words to go out of the world with! good as 'I still
live,' but on no razors.[1]

[1] Daniel Webster's last words were at one time etched on razors made by
Wade & Butcher of Sheffield.

### THE CONCORD COUNTRYMEN

*December* 3, 1856.   How I love the simple, reserved countrymen, my neighbors, who mind their own business and let me
alone, who never waylaid nor shot at me, to my knowledge,
when I crossed their fields, though each one has a gun in his
house!  For nearly twoscore years I have known, at a distance, these long-suffering men, whom I never spoke to,
who never spoke to me, and now feel a certain tenderness
for them, as if this long probation were but the prelude to an
eternal friendship.  What a long trial we have withstood, and
how much more admirable we are to each other, perchance,
than if we had been bedfellows!  I am not only grateful because Veias, and Homer, and Christ, and Shakespeare have
lived, but I am grateful for Minott, and Rice, and Melvin,
and Goodwin, and Puffer even.  I see Melvin all alone filling
his sphere, in russet suit, which no other could fill or suggest.
He takes up as much room in nature as the most famous.

### SALESMANSHIP

*December* 4, 1856.   When I bought my boots yesterday,
Hastings ran over his usual rigmarole.  Had he any stout
old-fashioned cowhide boots?  Yes, he thought he could suit
me. 'There's something that'll turn water about as well as
anything.  Billings had a pair just like them the other day,
and he said they kept his feet as dry as a bone.  But what's
more than that, they were made above a year ago upon
honor.  They are just the thing, you may depend on it.  I

had an eye to you when I was making them.' 'But they are too soft and thin for me. I want them to be thick and stand out from my foot.' 'Well, there is another pair, maybe a little thicker. I'll tell you what it is, these were made of dry hide.'

Both were warranted single leather and not split. I took the last. But after wearing them round this cold day I found that the little snow which rested on them and melted wet the upper leather through like paper and wet my feet, and I told H. of it, that he might have an offset to Billings's experience. 'Well, you can't expect a new pair of boots to turn water at first. I tell the farmers that the time to buy boots is at midsummer, or when they are hoeing their potatoes, and the pores have a chance to get filled with dirt.'


### THE PICKEREL-FISHERS


*December* 7, 1856. As I enter on Fair Haven Pond, I see already three pickerel-fishers retreating from it, drawing a sled through the Baker Farm, and see where they have been fishing, by the shining chips of ice about the holes. Others were here even yesterday, as it appears. The pond must have been frozen by the 4th at least. Some fisherman or other is ready with his reels and bait as soon as the ice will bear, whether it be Saturday or Sunday. Theirs, too, is a sort of devotion, though it be called hard names by the preacher, who perhaps could not endure the cold and wet any day. Perhaps he dines off their pickerel on Monday at the hotel. The ice appears to be but three or four inches thick.

## MINOTT'S WOOD-LOT

*December* 11, 1856. Minott tells me that his and his sister's wood-lot together contains about ten acres and has, with a very slight exception at one time, supplied all their fuel for thirty years, and he thinks would constantly continue to do so. They keep one fire all the time, and two some of the time, and burn about eight cords in a year. He knows his wood-lot and what grows in it as well as an ordinary farmer does his corn-field, for he has cut his own wood till within two or three years; knows the history of every stump on it and the age of every sapling; knows how many beech trees and black birches there are there, as another knows his pear or cherry trees. He complains that the choppers make a very long carf nowadays, doing most of the cutting on one

side, to avoid changing hands so much. It is more econom-
ical, as well as more poetical, to have a wood-lot and cut and
get out your own wood from year to year than to buy it at
your door. Minott may say to his trees: 'Submit to my axe.
I cut your father on this very spot.' How many sweet passages there must have been in his life there, chopping all
alone in the short winter days! How many rabbits, partridges, foxes he saw! A rill runs through the lot, where he
quenched his thirst, and several times he has laid it bare.
At last rheumatism has made him a prisoner, and he is compelled to let a stranger, a vandal, it may be, go into his lot
with an axe. It is fit that he should be buried there.

### PETER, THE PIG-BUTCHER

*December* 12, 1856. Yesterday morning I noticed that
several people were having their pigs killed, not foreseeing
the thaw. Such warm weather as this the animal heat will
hardly get out before night. I saw Peter, the dexterous pig-
butcher, busy in two or three places, and in the afternoon I
saw him with washed hands and knives in sheath and his
leather overalls drawn off, going to his solitary house on the
edge of the Great Fields, carrying in the rain a piece of the
pork he had slaughtered, with a string put through it. Often
he carries home the head, which is less prized, taking his
pay thus in kind, and these supplies do not come amiss to his
outcast family.

I saw Lynch's dog stealthily feeding at a half of his master's pig, which lay dressed on a wheelbarrow at the door. A
little yellow-brown dog, with fore feet braced on the ice and
outstretched neck, he eagerly browsed along the edge of the

meat, half a foot to right and left, with incessant short and rapid snatches, which brought it away as readily as if it had been pudding. He evidently knew very well that he was stealing, but made the most of his time. The little brown dog weighed a pound or two more afterward than before.

## LECTURING AT AMHERST, NEW HAMPSHIRE

*December* 18, 1856. At my lecture, the audience attended to me closely, and I was satisfied; that is all I ask or expect generally. Not one spoke to me afterward, nor needed they. I have no doubt that they liked it, in the main, though few of them would have dared say so, provided they were conscious of it. Generally, if I can only get the ears of an audience, I do not care whether they say they like my lecture or not. I think I know as well as they can tell. At any rate, it is none of my business, and it would be impertinent for me to inquire. The stupidity of most of these country towns, not to include the cities, is in its innocence infantile. Lectured in basement (vestry) of the orthodox church, and I trust helped to undermine it.

I was told to stop at the U. S. Hotel, but an old inhabitant had never heard of it and could not tell me where to find it, but I found the letters on a sign without help. It was the ordinary unpretending (?) desolate-looking country tavern. The landlord apologized to me because there was to be a ball there that night which would keep me awake, and it did. He and others there, horrible to relate, were in the habit of blowing their noses with their fingers and wiping them on their boots! Champney's U. S. Hotel was an ordinary team tavern, and the letters U. S., properly enough, not very conspicuous on the sign.

## THE WALDEN FISHERMEN

*December* 28, 1856.　The fishermen sit by their damp fire of rotten pine wood, so wet and chilly that even smoke in their eyes is a kind of comfort. There they sit, ever and anon scanning their reels to see if any have fallen, and, if not catching many fish, still getting what they went for, though they may not be aware of it, *i. e.* a wilder experience than the town affords.

## A DESERTED SERVANT

*January* 1, 1857.　Am still surveying the W—— or Lee farm. W—— cleared out and left this faithful servant like a cat in some corner of this great house, but without enough to buy him a pair of boots, I hear. Parker was once a Shaker at Canterbury. He is now Captain E——'s right-hand man. He found him in the house. P. does the chores. Complains that, as they dine at fashionable hours, he doesn't get enough to support him when he goes home at noon from helping me. When he sees how much dead wood there is on the farm, he says they ought to have a 'gundalo,' meaning a large, square kind of boat, to cart it off with.

E——, having lent W—— money, was obliged to take the farm to save himself, but he is nearly blind, and is anxious to get rid of it. Says that the buildings are either new or in excellent repair. He understands that in W——'s day they mixed paint by the hogshead. Parker has told him of logs cut two years ago which lie rotting in the swamp, and he is having them hauled out and to mill.

*January* 2.   To-day I see Parker is out with horse and cart, collecting dead wood at the Rock and drawing it home over the meadow.  I saw the English servant-girl with one of the children flat on the ice hard at work on the river cutting a hole with a hatchet, but, as the ice was thick and the water gushed up too soon for her, I saw that she would fail and directed her to an open place.  She was nearly beat out.  The hole, she said, was to drown a cat in; probably one which the W——s left behind as they did Parker.   E—— is resolved on a general clearing-up.

### GEORGE MINOTT

*January* 8, 1857.   Miss Minott tells me that she does not think her brother George has ever been to Boston more than once (though she tells me he says he has been twice),[1] and certainly not since 1812.  He was born in the Casey house, *i. e.* the same in which C. lived, the second of three that stood beyond the old black house beyond Moore's.  Casey was a Guinea negro.  Casey used to weep in his latter days when he thought of his wife and two children in Africa from whom he was kidnapped.  Minott went only to the East Quarter schools.  The house he now lives in is about sixty years old, was moved from beside Casey's to where it now stands before it was roofed.  Minott says he has lived where he now does as much as sixty years.  He has not been up in town for three years, on account of his rheumatism.  Does nothing whatever in the house but read the newspapers and few old books they have, the Almanac especially, and hold the cats, and very little indeed out of the house.  Is just able to saw and split the wood.

[1] *He* since tells me *once.*   [Thoreau's pencil note.]

## THE COLD FRIDAY

*January* 11, 1857.   Mother remembers the Cold Friday [1]
very well.  She lived in the house where I was born.  The
people in the kitchen — Jack Garrison, Esther, and a Hardy
girl — drew up close to the fire, but the dishes which the
Hardy girl was washing froze as fast as she washed them,
close to the fire.  They managed to keep warm in the parlor
by their great fires.

## RUNNING A LINE

*January* 11, 1857.   The other day a man came 'just to get
me to run a line in the woods.'  This is the usual request.  'Do
you know where one end of it is?'  I asked.  (It was the Strat-
ton lot.)  'No,' said he, 'I don't know either end; that is what
I want to find.'  'Do you know either of the next sides of the
lot?'  Thinking a moment, he answered, 'No.'  'Well, do
you know any one side of the whole lot, or any corner?'
After a little hesitation he said that he did not.  Here, then,
was a wood-lot of half a dozen acres, well enough described
in a deed dated 1777, courses and distances given, but he
could not tell exactly in what part of the universe any particular part of it was, but he expected me to find out.  This
was what he understood by 'running.'  On the strength of
this deed he had forbidden a man to chop wood somewhere.

Frequently, when my employer does not know where his
land lies, and has put into my hands an ancient and tattered

[1] January 19, 1810.

piece of paper called his deed, which throws no light at all on the question, he turns away, saying, 'I want you to make it all right. Give me all that belongs to me.'

### A BOY'S CAVE IN THE SNOW

*January* 20, 1857. At R. W. E.'s this evening, at about 6 P. M., I was called out to see Eddy's [1] cave in the snow. It was a hole about two and a half feet wide and six feet long, into a drift, a little winding, and he had got a lamp at the inner extremity. I observed, as I approached in a course at right angles with the length of the cave, that the mouth of the cave was lit as if the light were close to it, so that I did not suspect its depth. Indeed, the light of this lamp was remarkably reflected and distributed. The snowy walls were one universal reflector with countless facets. I think that one lamp would light sufficiently a hall built of this material. The snow about the mouth of the cave within had the yellow color of the flame to one approaching, as if the lamp were close to it. We afterward buried the lamp in a little crypt in this snow-drift and walled it in and found that its light was visible, even in this *twilight*, through fifteen inches' thickness of snow. The snow was all aglow with it. If it had been darker, probably it would have been visible through a much greater thickness. But, what was most surprising to me, when Eddy crawled into the extremity of his cave and shouted at the top of his voice, it sounded ridiculously faint, as if he were a quarter of a mile off, and at first I could not believe that he spoke loud, but we all of us crawled in by turns, and though our heads were only six feet from those

[1] Edward Waldo Emerson, the only son of the philosopher then living.

outside, our loudest shouting only amused and surprised them. Apparently the porous snow drank up all the sound.

## MINOTT ON THE COLD FRIDAY

*January* 22, 1857. I asked M[inott] about the Cold Friday. He said, 'It was plaguy cold; it stung like a wasp.' He remembers seeing them toss up water in a shoemaker's shop, usually a very warm place, and when it struck the floor it was frozen and rattled like so many shot. Old John Nutting used to say, 'When it is cold it is a sign it's going to be warm,' and 'When it's warm it's a sign it's going to be cold.'

## PRATT'S ADMIRABLE SIMPLICITY

*January* 27, 1857. Was struck to-day with the admirable simplicity of Pratt. He told me not only of the discovery of the tower of Babel, which, from the measures given, he had calculated could not stand between the roads at the Mill Pond, but of the skeleton of a man twenty feet long. Also of an eyestone which he has, bought of Betty Nutting, about as big as half a pea. Just lay it in your eye, bind up your eye with a handkerchief, and go to bed. It will not pain you, but you will feel it moving about, and when it has gathered all the dirt in the eye to itself, it will always come out, and you will probably find it in the handkerchief. It is a little thing and you must look sharp for it. He often lends his.

## WILLOW HEDGES

*February* 10, 1857.   Hayden, senior, tells me that when he lived with Abel Moore, Moore's son Henry one day set out a row of willow boughs for a hedge, but the father, who had just been eradicating an old willow-row at great labor and expense, asked Hayden who had done that and finally offered him a dollar if he would destroy them, which he agreed to do.  So each morning, as he went to and from his work, he used to pull some of them up a little way, and if there were many roots formed he rubbed them off on a rock.  And when, at the breakfast-table, Henry expressed wonder that his willows did not grow any better, being set in a rich soil, the father would look at Hayden and laugh.

## HOW TO CATCH A PIG [1]

*February* 15, 1857.   If it is a wild shoat, do not let him get scared; shut up the dogs and keep mischievous boys and men out of the way.  Think of some suitable inclosure in the neighborhood, no matter if it be a pretty large field, if it chances to be tightly fenced; and with the aid of another prudent person give the pig all possible opportunities to enter it.  Do not go very near him nor appear to be driving him, only let him avoid you, persuade him to prefer that inclosure.  If the case is desperate and it is necessary, you may make him think that you wish him to go anywhere else but into that field, and he will be pretty sure to go there.

[1] Thoreau's own heading.

Having got him into that inclosure and put up the fence, you can contract it at your leisure. When you have him in your hands, if he is obstinate, do not try to drive him with a rope round one leg. Spare the neighbors' ears and your pig's feelings, and put him into a cart or wheelbarrow.

### THE NEIGHBORS

*February* 19, 1857.   An old man, one of my neighbors, is so demented that he put both legs into one leg of his pantaloons the other morning!

Mr. Cheney tells me that Goodwin brought him a partridge to sell in the midst of the late severe weather. C. said it was a pity to kill it, it must find it hard to get a living. 'I guess she didn't find it any harder than I do,' answered G.

### A STRONG AND RESOLUTE MAN

*February* 20, 1857.   Minott always sits in the corner behind the door, close to the stove, with commonly the cat by his side, often in his lap. Often he sits with his hat on. He says that Frank Buttrick (who for a great many years worked at carpentering for John Richardson, and was working for him when he died) told him that Richardson called him when he was at the point of death and told him that he need not stop working on account of his death, but he might come in to the prayer if he wished to. R. is spoken of as a strong and resolute man.

### RICE'S POETIC LIFE

*March* 11, 1857. I see and talk with Rice, sawing off the ends of clapboards which he has planed, to make them square, for an addition to his house. He has got a fire in his shop, and plays at house-building there. His life is poetic. He does the work himself. He combines several qualities and talents rarely combined. Though he owns houses in the city, whose repair he attends to, finds tenants for them, and collects the rent, he also has his Sudbury farm and bean-fields. Though he lived in a city, he would still be natural and related to primitive nature around him. Though he owned all Beacon Street, you might find that his mittens were made of the skin of a woodchuck that had ravaged his bean-field, which he had cured. I noticed a woodchuck's skin tacked up to the inside of his shop. He said it had fatted on his beans, and William had killed it and expected to get another to make a pair of mittens of, one not being quite large enough. It was excellent for mittens. You could hardly wear it out.

### GOODWIN'S WOOD-PILE

*March* 18, 1857. I meet Goodwin paddling up the still, dark river on his first voyage to Fair Haven for the season, looking for muskrats and from time to time picking driftwood — logs and boards, etc. — out of the water and laying it up to dry on the bank, to eke out his wood-pile with. He says that the frost is not out so that he can lay wall, and so he thought he'd go and see what there was at Fair Haven. Says that when you hear a woodpecker's *rat-tat-tat-tat-tat* on a dead tree it is a sign of rain. While Emerson sits writing in his study this still, overcast, moist day, Goodwin is paddling up the still, dark river. Emerson burns twenty-five cords of wood and fourteen (?) tons of coal; Goodwin perhaps a cord and a half, much of which he picks out of the river. He says he'd rather have a boat leak some for fishing. I hear the report of his gun from time to time for an hour, heralding the death of a muskrat and reverberating far down the river.

### A TALK WITH THE BLACKSMITH

*March* 26, 1857. Stopped at Farrar's little stithy. He is making two nuts to mend a mop with, and when at length he

has forged and filed them and cut the thread, he remarks that it is a puttering job and worth a good deal more than he can charge. He has sickness in the house, a daughter in consumption, which he says is a flattering disease, up one day and down the next. Seeing a monstrous horseshoe nailed against his shop inside, with a little one within it, I asked what that was for. He said that he made the big one when he was an apprentice (of three months' standing) for a sign, and he picked up the little one the other day in the road and put it within it for the contrast. But he thought that the big one was hardly too big for one of the fore feet of the horse Columbus, which he had seen.

## A WAYFARING MAN

*April* 2, 1857. The other day as I came to the front of the house I caught sight of a genuine wayfaring man, an oldish countryman, with a frock and a bundle strapped to his back, who was speaking to the butcher, just then driving off in his cart. He was a gaunt man with a flashing eye, as if half crazy with travel, and was complaining, 'You see it shakes me so, I would rather travel the common road.' I supposed that he referred to the railroad, which the butcher had recommended for shortness. I was touched with compassion on observing the butcher's apparent indifference, as, jumping to his seat, he drove away before the traveller had finished his sentence, and the latter fell at once into the regular wayfarer's gait, bending under his pack and holding the middle of the road with a teetering gait.

## CATCHING SMELTS

*April* 11, 1857. 8 P. M. —Went to the Head of the River [1] to see them catch smelts. The water there is fresh when the tide is out. They use nets five or six feet square, stretched from the ends of crossed semicircular hoops, at the ends of poles about twelve feet long. The net bags down when raised. There were twenty or thirty fishermen standing close together, half on each side of the narrow river, each managing one of these nets, while a good part of the village appeared to be collected on the bridge. The tide was then coming in, but the best time is when it is going out. A fisherman told me that the smelt run up in the night only. These fishers stood just below a two-arched bridge. The tide was coming up between the arches, while the fresh water, which the smelt preferred, was running down next the shore on each side. The smelt were ascending in these streams of fresh water on each side. The shore for half a dozen rods on each side was lined with fishers, each wielding a single net. This man told me that the smelt had been running up about one month and were now about done. The herring had been seen for a fortnight. They will run this month and all the next. The former leave off when the latter begin. Shad have not been caught yet. They come after herring. Eels, too, are occasionally caught now, going up from the deeper river below. These fishes spawn in the little pond just above the bridge. They let the net rest on the bottom and every two or three minutes lift it up. They get thirty or many more smelt sometimes at one lift and catch other fish in the same way, even bass, sea perch, pickerel, eels, and sometimes a trout. The shad make

[1] The Acushnet River. Thoreau was visiting his friend Daniel Ricketson in New Bedford.

a ripple like a harrow, and you know when to raise the net. The villagers were talking across the stream, calling each other by their Christian names. Even mothers mingled with the fishermen, looking for their children. It suggested how much we had lost out of Concord River without realizing it. This is the critical season of a river, when it is fullest of life, its flowering season, the wavelets or ripples on its surface answering to the scales of the fishes beneath.

I saw the herring on sticks at the doors of many shops in New Bedford.

### THE WALDEN POND SOCIETY

*April* 16, 1857. About a month ago, at the post-office, Abel Brooks, who is pretty deaf, sidling up to me, observed in a loud voice which all could hear, 'Let me see, your society is pretty large, ain't it?' 'Oh, yes, large enough,' said I, not knowing what he meant. 'There's Stewart belongs to it, and Collier, he's one of them, and Emerson, and my boarder' (Pulsifer), 'and Channing, I believe, I think he goes there.' 'You mean the *walkers;* don't you?' 'Ye-es, I call you the Society. All go to the woods; don't you?' 'Do you miss any of your wood?' I asked. 'No, I hain't worried any yet. I believe you're a pretty clever set, as good as the average,' etc., etc.

Telling Sanborn [1] of this, he said that, when he first came to town and boarded at Holbrook's, he asked H. how many religious societies there were in town. H. said that there were three, — the Unitarian, the Orthodox, and the Walden Pond Society. I asked Sanborn with which Holbrook classed

[1] Frank B. Sanborn, who had then been living two years in Concord.

himself. He said he believes that he put himself with the last.

## AN ACTIVE MAN

*May* 4, 1857. Minott tells me of one Matthias Bowers, a native of Chelmsford and cousin of C. Bowers, a very active fellow, who used to sleep with him and when he found the door locked would climb over the roof and come in at the dormer-window. One Sunday, when they were repairing the old Unitarian church and there was a staging just above the belfry, he climbed up the lightning-rod and put his arm round the ball at the top of the spire and swung his hat there. He then threw it down and the crown was knocked out. Minott saw him do it, and Deacon White ordered him to come down. M. also told of a crazy fellow who got into the belfry of the Lincoln church with an axe and began to cut the spire down, but was stopped after he had done considerable damage.

## CORDUROY

*May* 8, 1857. Within a week I have had made a pair of corduroy pants, which cost when done $1.60. They are of that peculiar clay-color, reflecting the light from portions of their surface. They have this advantage, that, beside being very strong, they will look about as well three months hence as now, — or as ill, some would say. Most of my friends are disturbed by my wearing them. I can get four or five pairs for what one ordinary pair would cost in Boston, and each of the former will last two or three times as long under the same circumstances. The tailor said that the stuff was not made in this country; that it was worn by the Irish at home, and now they would not look at it, but others would not wear it, durable and cheap as it is, because it is worn by the Irish. Moreover, I like the color on other accounts. Anything but black clothes. I was pleased the other day to see a son of Concord return after an absence of eight years, not in a shining suit of black, with polished boots and a beaver or silk hat, as if on a furlough from human duties generally, — a mere clothes-horse, — but clad in an honest clay-colored suit and a snug every-day cap. It showed unusual manhood. Most returning sons come home dressed for the occasion.

## THE GENTLEMAN TRAVELLER

*June* 3, 1857. I have several friends and acquaintances who are very good companions in the house or for an afternoon walk, but whom I cannot make up my mind to make a longer excursion with; for I discover, all at once, that they are too gentlemanly in manners, dress, and all their habits. I see in my mind's eye that they wear black coats, considerable starched linen, glossy hats and shoes, and it is out of the question. It is a great disadvantage for a traveller to be a gentleman of this kind; he is so ill-treated, only a prey to landlords. It would be too much of a circumstance to enter a strange town or house with such a companion. You could not travel incognito; you might get into the papers. You should travel as a common man. If such a one were to set out to make a walking-journey, he would betray himself at every step. Every one would see that he was trying an experiment, as plainly as they see that a lame man is lame by his limping. The natives would bow to him, other gentlemen would invite him to ride, conductors would warn him that this was the second-class car, and many would take him for a clergyman; and so he would be continually pestered and balked and run upon. You would not see the natives at all. Instead of going in quietly at the back door and sitting by the kitchen fire, you would be shown into a cold parlor, there to confront a fireboard, and excite a commotion in a whole family. The women would scatter at your approach, and their husbands and sons would go right up to hunt up their black coats, — for they all have them; they are as cheap as dirt. You would go trailing your limbs along the highways, mere bait for corpulent innholders, as a pickerel's [*sic*] leg ¹ is trolled along a stream, and your part of the profits would be the frog's. No, you must be a common man, or at least travel as one, and then nobody will know that you are there or have been there. I would not undertake a simple pedestrian excursion with one of these, because to enter a village, or a hotel, or a private house, with such a one, would be too great a circumstance, would create too great a stir. You could only go half as far with the same means, for the price of. board and lodgings would rise everywhere; so much you have to pay for wearing that kind of coat. Not that the difference is in the coat at all, for the character of the scurf is determined by that of the true liber beneath. Innkeepers, stablers, conductors, clergymen, know a true wayfaring man at first sight and let him alone. It is of no use to shove your gaiter shoes a mile further than usual. Sometimes it is mere shiftlessness or want of originality, —

---

¹ The slip of the pen is obvious. A frog's leg was used for bait in trolling for pickerel.

the clothes wear them; sometimes it is egotism, that cannot afford to be treated like a common man, — they wear the clothes. They wish to be at least fully appreciated by every stage-driver and schoolboy. They would like well enough to see a new place, perhaps, but then they would like to be regarded as important public personages. They would consider it a misfortune if their names were left out of the published list of passengers because they came in the steerage, — an obscurity from which they might never emerge.

## DANIEL WEBSTER AND THE SEA-SERPENT

*June* 14, 1857.  B. M. Watson [1] tells me that he learns from pretty good authority that Webster once saw the sea-serpent. It seems it was first seen, in the bay between Manomet and Plymouth Beach, by a perfectly reliable witness (many years ago), who was accustomed to look out on the sea with his glass every morning the first thing as regularly as he ate his breakfast. One morning he saw this monster, with a head somewhat like a horse's raised some six feet above the water, and his body the size of a cask trailing behind. He was careering over the bay, chasing the mackerel, which ran ashore in their fright and were washed up and died in great numbers. The story is that Webster had appointed to meet some Plymouth gentlemen at Manomet and spend the day fishing with them. After the fishing was over, he set out to return to Duxbury in his sailboat with Peterson, as he had come, and on the way they saw the sea-serpent, which answered to the common account of this creature. It passed

[1] B. Marston Watson, of Plymouth. Thoreau had started for Cape Cod two days earlier and was spending a few days with him.

directly across their bows only six or seven rods off and then disappeared. On the sail homeward, Webster having had time to reflect on what had occurred, at length said to Peterson, 'For God's sake, never say a word about this to any one, for if it should be known that I have seen the sea-serpent, I should never hear the last of it, but wherever I went should have to tell the story to every one I met.' So it has not leaked out till now.

## GENERAL WINSLOW'S ADVENTURE

*June* 14, 1857. Watson tells me (and Ed. Watson [1] confirms it, his father having probably been of the party) that many years ago a party of Plymouth gentlemen rode round by the shore to the Gurnet and there had a high time. When they set out to return they left one of their number, a General Winslow, asleep, and as they rode along homeward, amused themselves with conjecturing what he would think when he waked up and found himself alone. When at length he awoke, he comprehended his situation at once, and, being somewhat excited by the wine he had drunk, he mounted his horse and rode along the shore to Saquish Head in the oppo-site direction. From here to the end of Plymouth Beach is about a mile and a quarter, but, it being low tide, he waded his horse as far as the beacon north of the channel, at the entrance to Plymouth Harbor, about three quarters of a mile, and then boldly swam him across to the end of Plymouth beach, about half a mile further, notwithstanding a strong current, and, having landed safely, he whipped up and soon reached the town, having come only about eight

[1] Edward Watson was Marston Watson's uncle.

miles, and had ample time to warm and dry himself at the tavern before his companions, who had at least twenty miles to ride about through Marshfield and Duxbury. And when they found him sitting by the tavern fire, they at first thought it was his ghost.


### A YOUNG PEDDLER


*June* 15, 1857. Mrs. Ellis [1] agreed to take me in, though they had already supped and she was unusually tired, it being washing-day. They were accustomed to put up peddlers from time to time, and had some pies just baked for such an emergency. At first took me for a peddler and asked what I carried in my bag. I was interested in a young peddler who soon after arrived and put up with his horse and cart, a simple and well-behaved boy of sixteen or seventeen only, peddling cutlery, who said that he started from Conway in this State. In answer to my question how he liked peddling, he said that he liked it on some accounts, it enabled him to see the world. I thought him an unusually good specimen of Young America. He found cutlery not good wares for that region; could do better where he came from, and was on his way to Boston for dry goods. Arranged to pay for his keeping partly in kind.

[1] Mrs. Samuel Ellis, of Plymouth.

## THE SHORTEST WAY

*June* 16, 1857.   With my chart and compass I can generally find a shorter way than the inhabitants can tell me.[1]   I stop at a depot a little one side of a village and ask the way to some place I am bound to.   The landlords and stage-drivers would fain persuade me to go first down on to the main street and follow that a piece; and when I show them a shorter way on the map, which leaves their village on one side, they shrug their shoulders, and say they would rather go round than get over the fences.   I have found the compass and chart safer guides than the inhabitants, though the latter universally abuse the maps.   I do not love to go through a village street any more than a cottage yard.   I feel that I am there only by sufferance; but I love to go by the villages by my own road, seeing them from one side, as I do theoretically.   When I go through a village, my legs ache at the prospect of the hard gravelled walk.   I go by the tavern with its porch full of gazers, and meet a miss taking a walk or the doctor in his sulky, and for half an hour I feel as strange as if I were in a town in China; but soon I am at home in the wide world again, and my feet rebound from the yielding turf.

## A DEAD MAN'S COAT

*June* 18, 1857.   A youngish man came into Small's[2] with a thick outside coat, when a girl asked where he got that coat. He answered that it was taken off a man that came ashore

---

[1] That is, on Cape Cod.          [2] In North Truro on Cape Cod.

dead, and he had worn it a year or more. The girls or young ladies expressed surprise that he should be willing to wear it and said, 'You'd not dare to go to sea with that coat on.' But he answered that he might just as well embark in that coat as any other.

## PROVINCETOWN NIGHTS

*June* 21, 1857. At the Pilgrim House, though it was not crowded, they put me into a small attic chamber which had two double beds in it, and only one window, high in a corner, twenty and a half inches by twenty-five and a half, in the alcove when it was swung open, and it required a chair to look out conveniently. Fortunately it was not a cold night and the window could be kept open, though at the risk of being visited by the cats, which appear to swarm on the roofs of Provincetown like the mosquitoes on the summits of its hills. I have spent four memorable nights there in as many different years, and have added considerable thereby to my knowledge of the natural history of the cat and the bedbug. Sleep was out of the question. A night in one of the attics of Provincetown! to say nothing of what is to be learned in entomology. It would be worth the while to send a professor there, one who was also skilled in entomology. Such is your *Pilgerruhe* or Pilgrims'-Rest. Every now and then one of these animals on its travels leaped from a neighboring roof on to mine, with such a noise as if a six-pounder had fallen within two feet of my head, — the discharge of a catapult, — a twelve-pounder discharged by a catapult, — and then followed such a scrambling as banished sleep for a long season, while I watched lest they came in at the open window. A kind of foretaste, methought, of the infernal regions. I didn't wonder they gave quit-claim deeds of their land here. My experience is that you fare best at private houses. The barroom may be defined a place to spit.

> 'Soon as the evening shades prevail,
> The *cats take* up the wondrous tale.'

At still midnight, when, half awake, half asleep, you seem to be weltering in your own blood on a battlefield, you hear the stealthy tread of padded feet belonging to some animal of the cat tribe, perambulating the roof within a few inches of your head.

### A COLLECTION OF EGGS

*June* 24, 1857. Looked over Farmer's [1] eggs and list of names. He has several which I have not. Is not his 'chick-lisee,' after all, the Maryland yellow-throat? The eggs were numbered with a pen, — 1, 2, 3, etc., — and corresponding numbers written against the names on the cover of the pasteboard box in which were the eggs. Among the rest I read, *'Fire never redder.'* That must be the tanager. He laughed and said that this was the way he came to call it by that name: Many years ago, one election-day, when he and other boys, or young men, were out gunning to see how many birds they could kill, Jonathan Hildreth, who lived near by, saw one of these birds on the top of a tree before him in the woods, but he did not see a deep ditch that crossed his course between him and it. As he raised his gun, he exclaimed, 'Fire never redder!' and, taking a step or two forward, with his eye fixed on the bird, fell headlong into the ditch, and so the name became a byword among his fellows.

[1] Jacob Farmer, who lived on the Lowell road.

## PROFANITY

*August* 28, 1857. As we were riding by Deacon Farrar's lately, E. Hoar [1] told me in answer to my questions, that both the young Mr. Farrars, who had now come to man's estate, were excellent young men, — their father, an old man of about seventy, once cut and corded seven cords of wood in one day, and still cut a double swath at haying time, and was a man of great probity, — and to show the unusual purity of one of them, at least, he said that, his brother Frisbie, [2] who had formerly lived there, inquiring what had become of a certain hired man whom he used to know, young Mr. Farrar told him that he was gone, 'that the truth was he one day let drop a prophane word, and after that he thought that he could not have him about, and so he got rid of him.' It was as if he had dropped some filthy thing on the premises, an intolerable nuisance, only to be abated by removing the source of it. I should like to hear as good news of the New England farmers generally. It to some extent accounts for the vigor of the father and the successful farming of the sons.

## A VETERAN OF THE REVOLUTION

*August* 28, 1857. I read the other day in the *Tribune* that a man apparently about seventy, and smart at that, went

[1] Edward Hoar, with whom Thoreau had recently made his third trip to the Maine woods.

[2] George Frisbie Hoar, afterwards well known as United States Senator from Massachusetts.

to the police in New York and asked for a lodging, having
been left by the cars or steamboat when on his way to Connecticut. When they asked his age, native place, etc., he
said his name was McDonald; he was born in Scotland in
1745, came to Plymouth, Mass., in 1760, was in some battles
in the Revolution, in which he lost an eye; had a son eighty-
odd years old, etc.; but, seeing a reporter taking notes, he
was silent. Since then I heard that an old man named
McDonald, one hundred and twelve years old, had the day
before passed through Concord and was walking to Lexington, and I said at once he must be a humbug. When I went
to the post-office to-night (August 28), G. Brooks asked me if
I saw him and said that he heard that he told a correct story,
except he said that he remembered Braddock's defeat! He
had noticed that Dr. Heywood's old house, the tavern, was
gone since he was here in the Revolution. Just then Davis,
the postmaster, asked us to look at a letter he had received.
It was from a Dr. Curtis of Newton asking if this McDonald
belonged about Concord as he said, and saying that his story
appeared to be a correct one. Davis had never heard of him,
and, as we presumed him to be a humbug, we advised Davis
to write accordingly. But I afterward remembered reading
nearly a year ago of a man of this name and age in St. Louis,
who said he had married a wife in Concord before the Revolution, and then began to think that his story might be all
true. So it seems that a veteran of a hundred and twelve,
after an absence of eighty-seven years, may come back to
the town where he married his wife in order to hunt up his
relatives, and not only have no success, but be pronounced
a humbug!!

## WYMAN AND THE CROW

*September* 30, 1857.   Minott said that as he was going over to Lincoln one day thirty or forty years ago, taking his way through Ebby Hubbard's woods, he heard a great flock of crows cawing over his head, and one alighted just within gunshot. He raised his little gun marked London, which he knew would fetch down anything that was within gunshot, and down came the crow; but he was not killed, only so filled with shot that he could not fly. As he was going by John Wyman's at the pond, with the live crow in his hand, Wyman asked him what he was going to do with that crow, to which he answered, 'Nothing in particular,' — he happened to alight within gunshot, and so he shot him. Wyman said

that he'd like to have him. 'What do you want to do with him?' asked M. 'If you'll give him to me, I'll tell you,' said the other. To which Minott said, 'You may have him and welcome.' Wyman then proceeded to inform him that the crows had eaten a great space in Josh Jones the blacksmith's corn-field, which Minott had passed just below the alms-house, and that Jones had told him that if he could kill a crow in his corn-field he would give him half a bushel of rye. He could guess what he wanted the crow for. So Wyman took the crow and the next time he went into town he tossed him over the wall into the corn-field and then shot him, and, carrying the dead crow to Jones, he got his half-bushel of rye.

### MINOTT'S STORY-TELLING

*October* 2, 1857. The chief incidents in Minott's life must be more distinct and interesting to him now than immediately after they occurred, for he has recalled and related them so often that they are stereotyped in his mind. Never having travelled far from his hillside, he does not suspect himself, but tells his stories with fidelity and gusto to the minutest details, — as much as Herodotus his histories.

### WALKING ROUND THE SQUARE

*October* 3, 1857. Getting over the wall near Sam Barrett's the other day, I had gone a few rods in the road when I met Prescott Barrett, who observed, 'Well, you take a walk round the square sometimes.' So little does he know of my habits. I go across lots over his grounds every three or four weeks, but I do not know that I ever walked round the square in my life.

### A CHEERY OLD MAN

*October* 20, 1857. I had gone but little way on the old Carlisle road when I saw Brooks Clark, who is now about eighty and bent like a bow, hastening along the road, bare-footed, as usual, with an axe in his hand; was in haste perhaps on account of the cold wind on his bare feet. It is he who took the *Centinel* so long. When he got up to me, I saw that besides the axe in one hand, he had his shoes in the other, filled with knurly apples and a dead robin. He stopped and talked with me a few moments; said that we had had a noble autumn and might now expect some cold weather. I asked if he had found the robin dead. No, he said, he found it with its wing broken and killed it. He also added that he had found some apples in the woods, and as he hadn't anything to carry them in, he put 'em in his shoes. They were queer-looking trays to carry fruit in. How many he got in along toward the toes, I don't know. I noticed, too, that his pockets were stuffed with them. His old tattered frock coat was hanging in strips about the skirts, as were his pantaloons about his naked feet. He appeared to have been out on a scout this gusty afternoon, to see what he could find, as the youngest boy might. It pleased me to see this cheery old man, with such a feeble hold on life, bent almost double, thus enjoying the evening of his days. Far be it from me to call it avarice or penury, this childlike delight in finding

# PLATE IX

*Barefooted Brooks Clark Building Wall*

something in the woods or fields and carrying it home in the October evening, as a trophy to be added to his winter's store. Oh, no; he was happy to be Nature's pensioner still, and birdlike to pick up his living. Better his robin than your turkey, his shoes full of apples than your barrels full; they will be sweeter and suggest a better tale. He can afford to tell how he got them, and we to listen. There is an old wife, too, at home, to share them and hear how they were obtained. Like an old squirrel shuffling to his hole with a nut. Far less pleasing to me the loaded wain, more suggestive of avarice and of spiritual penury.

This old man's cheeriness was worth a thousand of the church's sacraments and *memento mori*'s. It was better than a prayerful mood. It proves to me old age as tolerable, as happy, as infancy. I was glad of an occasion to suspect that this afternoon he had not been at 'work' but living somewhat after my own fashion (though he did not explain the axe), — had been out to see what nature had for him, and now was hastening home to a burrow he knew, where he could warm his old feet. If he had been a young man, he would probably have thrown away his apples and put on his shoes when he saw me coming, for shame. But old age is manlier; it has learned to live, makes fewer apologies, like infancy. This seems a very manly man. I have known him within a few years building stone wall by himself, barefooted.

### MELVIN'S NUTTING

*October* 20, 1857. There was Melvin, too, a-barberrying and nutting. He had got two baskets, one in each hand, and his game-bag, which hung from his neck, all full of nuts and barberries, and his mouth full of tobacco. Trust him to find where the nuts and berries grow. He is hunting all the year and he marks the bushes and the trees which are fullest, and when the time comes, for once leaves his gun, though not his dog, at home, and takes his baskets to the spot. It is pleasanter to me to meet him with his gun or with his baskets than to meet some portly caterer for a family, basket on arm, at the stalls of Quincy Market. Better Melvin's pignuts than the others' shagbarks. It is to be observed that the best things are generally most abused, and so are not so much enjoyed as the worst. Shagbarks are eaten by epicures with diseased appetites; pignuts by the country boys who gather them. So fagots and rubbish yield more comfort than sound wood.

Melvin says he has caught partridges in his hands. If there's only one hole, knows they've not gone out. Sometimes shoots them through the snow.

### SAL CUMMINGS

*October* 23, 1857. Sal Cummings, a thorough countrywoman, conversant with nuts and berries, calls the soapwort gentian 'blue vengeance,' mistaking the word. A masculine wild-eyed woman of the fields. Somebody has her daguerreotype. When Mr. —— was to lecture on Kansas, she was sure 'she wa'n't going to hear him. None of her folks had ever had any.'

## THE LITTLETON GIANT

*October* 27, 1857.  The Littleton Giant brought us a load of coal within the week. He appears deformed and weakly, though naturally well formed. He does not nearly stand up straight. His knees knock together; they touch when he is standing most upright, and so reduce his height at least three inches. He is also very round-shouldered and stooping, probably from the habit of crouching to conceal his height. He wears a low hat for the same purpose. The tallest man looks like a boy beside him. He has a seat to his wagon made on purpose for him. He habitually stops before all doors. You wonder what his horses think of him, — that a strange horse is not afraid of him. His voice is deep and full, but mild, for he is quite modest and retiring, — really a worthy man, 'tis said. Pity he couldn't have been undertaken by a committee in season and put through, like the boy Safford,[1] been well developed bodily and also mentally, taught to hold up his head and not mind people's eyes or remarks. It is remarkable that the giants have never correspondingly great hearts.

### MINOTT'S TIMIDITY

*November* 5, 1857.  Minott was rather timid. One day early in the winter he had been over to Fair Haven Hill after a fox with John Wyman, but they didn't get him. The pond was

[1] Truman Henry Safford (1836–1901), mathematician and astronomer, who began life as an infant prodigy.

frozen about two inches thick, but you could easily see the water through the ice, and when they came back, Wyman said he was going straight across because it was nearer, but Minott objected. But Wyman told him to follow; it was safe enough. Minott followed half a dozen rods and then decided that he wouldn't risk it and went back; he'd go ten miles round sooner than cross. 'But,' said Minott, 'the fellow kept on and I'll be hanged if he didn't get safe across.'

### DR. RIPLEY'S PORK BARREL

*November* 6, 1857. Stedman Buttrick tells me that Dr. Ripley used to have his pork packed with the best pieces at the top of the barrel, and when some parishioner wondered at it, that he should thus eat these first, he answered that when packed thus the topmost were the best all the way through.

### BROOKS CLARK'S REMINISCENCES

*November* 6, 1857. When I came out on to the old Carlisle road in the dusk on my return, I saw Brooks Clark coming homeward, with his axe in his hand and both hands behind his back, being bent almost double. He said he was over eighty. Some years ago he bought some land up that way, and, the birches having sprung up there, he called it his birch pasture. There was enough birch wood there to carry him through the winter, and he was now cutting it. He remem-

bered when they began to burn lime there, and bought the
right to get out stone of Easterbrooks more than sixty years
ago. It was Peter Barrett that began it. The lime sold for
$5.00 a cask (larger casks than now). But the stone was
difficult to get out. He remembers seeing the mowers at
work in the meadow where Stedman Buttrick's handsome
pine and maple wood is, seventy years ago, and where there
was a large old chestnut by the roadside there, which being
cut, two sprouts came up which have become the largest
chestnut trees by the wall now. As for the yellow birch
cellar-hole, Ephraim Brown told him that old Henry Flint
(an ancestor of Clark's wife) dug it, and erected the frame
of a house there, but never finished it, selling out, going to
live by the river. It was never finished. Clark's father told
him that he remembered when there were no fences between
his house and Lawrence's; it was all open. This road was the
new one; the bridle-road the old one.

## MINOTT AND HIS COMRADES

*November* 6, 1857. Minott is a very pleasing figure in nature. He improves every scenery, — he and his comrades,
Harry Hooper, John Wyman, Oliver Williams, etc. If he
gets into a pond-hole he disturbs it no more than a water-
spirit for me.

*November* 7, 1857. Minott adorns whatever part of nature he touches; whichever way he walks he transfigures the
earth for me. If a common man speaks of Walden Pond to
me, I see only a shallow, dull-colored body of water without
reflections or peculiar color, but if Minott speaks of it, I

see the green water and reflected hills at once, for he *has been* there. I hear the rustle of the leaves from woods which he goes through.

### THE BOY AND THE BOUND

*November* 9, 1857. Surveying for Stedman Buttrick and Mr. Gordon. Jacob Farmer says that he remembers well a particular bound (which is the subject of dispute between the above two men) from this circumstance: He, a boy, was sent, as the representative of his mother, to witness the placing of the bounds to her lot, and he remembers that, when they had fixed the stake and stones, old Mr. Nathan Barrett asked him if he had a knife about him, upon which he pulled out his knife and gave it to him. Mr. Barrett cut a birch switch and trimmed it in the presence of young Farmer, and then called out, 'Boy, here's your knife;' but as the boy saw that he was going to strike him when he reached his hand for the knife, he dodged into a bush which alone received the blow. And Mr. Barrett said that if it had not been for that, he would have got a blow which would have made him remember that bound as long as he lived, and explained to him that that was his design in striking him. He had before told his mother that since she could not go to the woods to see what bounds were set to her lot, she had better send Jacob as a representative of the family. This made Farmer the important witness in this case. He first, some years ago, saw Buttrick trimming up the trees, and told him he was on Gordon's land and pointed out this as the bound between them.

One of the company to-day told of George Melvin once

directing Jonas Melvin, for a joke, to go to the widow Hildreth's lot (along which we were measuring) and gather the chestnuts. They were probably both working there. He accordingly took the oxen and cart and some ladders and another hired man, and they worked all day and got half a bushel.

A BOUNDARY DISPUTE

*November* 13, 1857.   My assistants and company in surveying on the 9th were, Gordon and Buttrick, the principals in the dispute; Jacob Farmer, the principal witness; George Buttrick, son of Stedman; and French, son-in-law of Gordon. I had the most to do with Gordon, who came after me. He was quite eloquent at our house on the subject of two neighbors disputing at his time of life about a 'pelfry' sum or a few rods of land; seemed really to have a very good heart; thought that the main thing in this life was to keep up friendly relations; and as he rode along, would quote Scripture in a low tone, and put his whole soul into some half-whispered expression which I could not hear, but nevertheless nodded assent to. He thought it was too bad that he should have spent his seventy-third birthday settling that dispute in the woods. Apparently did not know it till afterwards.

Buttrick is a rather large man, in more senses than one. His portly body as he stood over the bound was the mark at which I sighted through the woods, rather too wide a one for accuracy. He did not cease to regret for a day or two that I should have had no dinner, but Gordon detained me. Buttrick said that he had a piece of meat cooked and expected me at his house. Thought it too bad in Gordon to make a man go without his dinner, etc. He offered me a glass of gin, or wine, as I chose. Lamented the cutting down of apple orchards and scarcity of cider-mills. Told of an orchard in the town of Russell, on the side of a hill, where the apples rolled down and lay four feet deep (?) against a wall on the lower side, and this the owner cut down.

Farmer, half a dozen years since, saw Buttrick trimming up the trees there and observed to him, 'You are on Mr. Gordon's land.' This was the beginning of the trouble. Buttrick adhered to the bounds which Abel Brooks, who sold to him, had pointed out. Farmer was sure of the bounds between them, because when Jacob Brown's Bateman woodlot was divided between Mrs. Farmer (his mother) and her sister, the mother of Mrs. Gordon, he had witnessed the setting of the bounds as the representative of his mother, and came near being whipped at this one.

### 'CAPTAIN ABEL DAVIS'

*November* 14, 1857. It seems that the Abel Davis who caught the pickerel in Temple Brook, which would make such a meal for his 'Lavinia' and himself, was addicted to talking to himself, thinking aloud. He was once talked of for captain of the company, and about that time, they say, was overheard saying to himself, 'Captain Abel Davis! What a fine-looking man!'

## HARD WORK AND CHEERFULNESS

*November* 18, 1857. Flannery is the hardest-working man I know. Before sunrise and long after sunset he is taxing his unweariable muscles. The result is a singular cheerfulness. He is always in good spirits. He often overflows with his joy when you perceive no occasion for it. If only the gate sticks, some of it bubbles up and overflows in his passing comment on that accident. How much mere industry proves! There is a sparkle often in his passing remark, and his voice is really like that of a bird.

## CONVENIENT STUTTERING

*November* 26, 1857. Rice tells me he remembers that Nathan Barrett's father used to stutter. He went round collecting the direct taxes soon after the Revolution, — on carriages, watches, dogs, etc., etc. It was perhaps a dollar on a dog. Coming to Captain Bent's, who kept tavern in Sudbury where Israel Rice lives, he collected his tax and then said, 'I want you to may-ma-ma-ma-make me a ha-ha-ha-ha-ha — to make me a ha-ha-ha — a *whole* mug o' flip.'

THE GROWTH OF A RUMOR

*November* 29, 1857.  A week or so ago, as I learn, Miss
Emeline Barnett told a little boy who boards with her, and
who was playing with an open knife in his hand, that he
must be careful not to fall down and cut himself with it, for
once Mr. David Loring, when he was a little boy, fell down
with a knife in his hand and cut his throat badly.  It was
soon reported, among the children at least, that little David
Loring, the grandson of the former, had fallen down with a
knife in his hand as he was going to school, and nearly cut
his throat; next, that Mr. David Loring the grandfather
(who lives in Framingham) had committed suicide, had cut
his throat, was not dead, indeed, but was not expected to
live; and in this form the story spread like wildfire over the
town and county.  Nobody expressed surprise.  His oldest
acquaintances and best friends, his legal adviser, all said,
'Well, I can believe it.'  He was known by many to have been
speculating in Western lands, which, owing to the hard
times, was a failure, and he was depressed in consequence.
Sally Cummings helped spread the news.  Said there was no
doubt of it, but there was Fay's wife (L.'s daughter) knew
nothing of it yet, they were as merry as crickets over there.
Others stated that Wetherbee, the expressman, had been
over to Northboro, and learned that Mr. Loring had taken
poison in Northboro.  Mr. Rhodes was stated to have received a letter from Mr. Robbins of Framingham giving all
the particulars.  Mr. Wild, it was said, had also got a letter
from his son Silas in Framingham, to whom he had written,
which confirmed the report.  As Wild went down-town, he
met Meeks the carpenter and inquired in a significant way
if he got anything new.  Meeks simply answered, 'Well,

David Loring won't eat another Thanksgiving dinner.' A child at school wrote to her parents at Northboro, telling the news. Mrs. Loring's sister lives there, and it chances that her husband committed suicide. They were, therefore, slow to communicate the news to her, but at length could not contain themselves longer and told it. The sister was terribly affected; wrote to her son (L.'s nephew) in Worcester, who immediately took the cars and went to Framingham and when he arrived there met his uncle just putting his family into the cars. He shook his hand very heartily indeed, looking, however, hard at his throat, but said not a word about his errand. Already doubts had arisen, people were careful how they spoke of it, the expressmen were mum, Adams and Wetherbee never said Loring. The Framingham expressman used the same room with Adams in Boston. A. simply asked, 'Any news from Framingham this morning? Seen Loring lately?' and learned that all was well.

STAPLES'S PROSPERITY

*December* 8, 1857. Staples says he came to Concord some twenty-four years ago a poor boy with a dollar and three cents in his pocket, and he spent the three cents for drink at Bigelow's tavern, and now he's worth 'twenty hundred dollars clear.' He remembers many who inherited wealth whom he can buy out to-day. I told him that he had done better than I in a pecuniary respect, for I had only earned my living. 'Well,' said he, 'that's all I've done, and I don't know as I've got much better clothes than you.' I was particularly poorly clad then, in the woods; my hat, pants, boots, rubbers, and gloves would not have brought fourpence, and I told the Irishman that it wasn't everybody could afford to have a fringe round his legs, as I had, my corduroys not preserving a selvage.

Staples said there was one thing he liked. 'What is that?' 'An honest man.' If he lent a man money, and when it became due he came and asked for more time because he could not pay, he excused him, but if, after it had become due, he went to the man, and he then made the same excuse, he lost all confidence in him.

## AN ANECDOTE OF MRS. HOAR

*December* 13, 1857. I hear a characteristic anecdote respecting Mrs. Hoar, from good authority. Her son Edward, who takes his father's place and attends to the same duties, asked his mother the other night, when about retiring, 'Shall I put the cat down cellar?' 'No,' said she, 'you may put her outdoors.' The next night he asked, 'Shall I put the cat outdoors?' 'No,' answered she, 'you may put her down cellar.' The third night he asked, 'Shall I put the cat down cellar or outdoors?' 'Well,' said his mother, 'you may open the cellar door and then open the front door, and let her go just which way she pleases.' Edward suggested that it was a cold night for the cat to be outdoors, but his mother said, 'Who knows but she has a little kitten somewhere to look after?' Mrs. H. is a peculiar woman, who has her own opinion and way, a strong-willed, managing woman.

## COMPANIONS IN SURVEYING

*December* 31, 1857. I have been surveying most of the time for a month past and have associated with various characters: —

First there was Staples, quick, clear, downright, and on the whole a good fellow, especially good to treat with rougher and slower men than himself, always meaning well.

An Irishman, rather slow and dull but well-meaning.

A rustic innkeeper, evidently rather close-fisted.

George Heywood, a quiet, efficient man, very gentlemanly and agreeable to deal with; no pretense nor bluster, but simple, direct, and even sweet.

—— ——, a crooked stick, not readily apprehending your drift, referring to old deeds or places which he can't find, thinking he is entitled to many more acres than belong to him, but never leaving his work or his cattle to attend to you. To be found commonly in his barn, if you come upon him suddenly before he can hide. Has some complaint or injury which deforms him somewhat, — has crooked his body, so that when you meet him in the street he looks as if he was going across the road.

Another Irishman, one of the worst of his race, full of blarney, one of the would-be gentlemen, who, when treated according to his deserts, having complained unreasonably of my price, apologizes by saying that he meant nothing. 'What's the use of having a tongue in your head if you don't use it?'

A common specimen of the Yankee, who commonly answers me with 'exactly' or 'just so.'

—— ——, who was so afraid he should lose some land belonging to him that, though he had employed Rice to sur-

vey his small wood-lot of three acres, within a year, he working two or three days at it and setting at least fifty stakes
about it, having also two plans of it, yet, seeing that I had
by chance set a stake a foot or two one side of his line,
thought there was some mistake and would have me measure
his lot anew. It was but little labor, the lines were so open,
— for a path was actually worn round the whole lot. He
appears to go round it every day or two. When I wanted a
straight pole, he was very scrupulous not to cut it from his
neighbor's side of the line. He did not seem able to understand a plan or deed, and had sold some of his land because
he did not know that he had a good title to it. Everything
I told him about his deed and plan seemed to surprise him
infinitely and make him laugh with excess of interest. When
I pointed out anything in the plan, he did not look at it,
only at my finger and at me, and took my word for it. I
told him that I wondered his last surveyor had not set a
stake and stone in one place, according to his plan and

deed, a perfectly plain case, the stump of the pitch pine referred to being left. He said he didn't want to make bounds, and asked me if I should have set it there, to which I answered, 'Yes, of course,' that was what I had been doing all my life, making bounds, or rather finding them, remaking what had been unmade, where they were away. He listened to me as if I were an oracle. He did not in the least understand my instrument, or 'spy-glass,' as he called it, but had full faith that it knew the way straight through the thickest wood to missing bounds. He was so deaf I had to shout to him, and there were two more in his house deafer than he, — and I think only one other. The passers-by commonly hear them talking to one another within. I could never communicate with him when setting a stake or carrying the chain but by signs, and must first get his attention to the signs. This I accomplished, when he had hold of the chain, by giving it several smart jerks. When he paid me at his house, I observed that all his money was in silver. He said he told H—— that we had been cutting off some of his land, and H—— said, 'Is that right?' H—— has a good deal of large old wood which he will not cut. —— says that he goes into it with his axe, and striking on an old tree says, 'That's sound,' and so lets it stand, though when cut it turns out to be false-hearted.

—— says that Rice worked two days on only two sides of his lot, but that he told him he would not charge him but two dollars if it took him a week. I found and used one of Rice's poles, left on the ground all planed for the purpose, for he worked not without tools.

### LECTURING IN LYNN

*January* 13, 1858.   Go to Lynn to lecture, *via* Cambridge.

4.30 P. M. — At Jonathan Buffum's, Lynn.   Lecture in John B. Alley's parlor.   Mr. J. Buffum describes to me ancient wolf-traps, made probably by the early settlers in Lynn, perhaps after an Indian model; one some two miles from the shore near Saugus, another more northerly; holes say seven feet deep, about as long, and some three feet wide, stoned up very smoothly, and perhaps converging a little, so that the wolf could not get out.   Tradition says that a wolf and a squaw were one morning found in the same hole, staring at each other.

### LYNN AND NAHANT

*January* 14, 1858.   Mr. Buffum says that in 1817 or 1819 he saw the sea-serpent at Swampscott, and so did several hundred others.   He was to be seen off and on for some time. There were many people on the beach the first time, in carriages partly in the water, and the serpent came so near that they, thinking that he might come ashore, involuntarily turned their horses to the shore as with a general consent, and this movement caused him to shear off also.   The road from Boston was lined with people directly, coming to see the monster.   Prince came with his spy-glass, saw, and printed his account of him.   Buffum says he has seen him twenty times, once alone, from the rocks at Little Nahant, when he passed along close to the shore just beneath the surface, and within fifty or sixty feet of him, so that he could have touched him with a very long pole, if he had dared to. Buffum is about sixty, and it should be said, as affecting the value of his evidence, that he is a firm believer in Spiritualism.

This forenoon I rode to Nahant with Mr. Buffum. All the country bare. A fine warm day; neither snow nor ice, unless you search narrowly for them. On the way we pass Mr. Alonzo Lewis's cottage. On the top of each of his stone posts is fastened a very perfectly egg-shaped pebble of sienite from Kettle Cove, fifteen to eighteen inches long and of proportionate diameter. I never saw any of that size so perfect. There are some fifteen of them about his house, and on one flatter, circular one he has made a dial, by which I learned the hour (9.30 A. M.). Says he was surveying once at Kettle Cove, where they form a beach a third of a mile long and two to ten feet deep, and he brought home as many as his horse could draw. His house is clapboarded with hemlock bark; now some twenty years old. He says that he built it himself.

Called at the shop where lately Samuel Jillson, now of Feltonville, set up birds, — for he is a taxidermist and very skillful; kills his own birds and with blow-guns, which he makes and sells, some seven feet long, of glass, using a clay ball. Is said to be a dead shot at six rods!

MINOTT'S EAR FOR BIRD-NOTES

*January* 28, 1858. Minott has a sharp ear for the note of any migrating bird. Though confined to his dooryard by the rheumatism, he commonly hears them sooner than the widest rambler. Maybe he listens all day for them, or they come and sing over his house, — report themselves to him and receive their season ticket. He is never at fault. If he says he heard such a bird, though sitting by his chimney-side, you may depend on it. He can hear through glass. He has not spoiled his ears by attending lectures and caucuses, etc. The other day the rumor went that a flock of geese had been seen flying north over Concord, midwinter as it was, by the almanac. I traced it to Minott, and yet I was compelled to doubt. I had it directly that he had heard them within a week. I saw him, — I made haste to him. His reputation was at stake. He said that he stood in his shed, — it was one of the late warm, muggy, April-like mornings, — when he heard one short but distinct *honk* of a goose. He went into the house, he took his cane, he exerted himself, or that sound imparted strength to him. Lame as he was, he went up on to the hill, — he had not done it for a year, — that he might hear all around. He saw nothing, but he heard the note again. It came from over the brook. It was a wild goose, he was sure of it. And hence the rumor spread and grew. He thought that the back of the winter was broken, — if it had any this year, — but he feared such a winter would kill him too.

I was silent; I reflected; I drew into my mind all its members, like the tortoise; I abandoned myself to unseen guides. Suddenly the truth flashed on me, and I remembered that within a week I had heard of a box at the tavern, which had come by railroad express, containing three wild geese and directed to his neighbor over the brook. The April-like morning had excited one so that he honked; and Minott's reputation acquired new lustre.

He has a propensity to tell stories which you have no ears to hear, which you cut short and return unfinished upon him.

## A CONCORD NEGRO SLAVE

*February* 18, 1858.  George Minott tells me that he, when young, used often to go to a store by the side of where Bigelow's tavern was and kept by Ephraim Jones, — the Goodnow store. That was probably the one kept by my old trader. Told me how Casey, who was a slave to a man — Whitney — who lived where Hawthorne owns, — the same house, — before the Revolution, ran off one Sunday, was pursued by the neighbors, and hid himself in the river up to his neck till nightfall, just across the Great Meadows. He ran through Gowing's Swamp and came back that night to a Mrs. Cogswell, who lived where Charles Davis does, and got something to eat; then cleared far away, enlisted, and was freed as a soldier after the war. Whitney's boy threw snowballs at him the day before, and finally C., who was chopping in the yard, threw his axe at him, and W. said he was an ugly nigger and he must put him in jail. He may have been twenty years old when stolen from Africa; left a wife and one child there. Used to say that he went home to Africa in the night and came back again in the morning; *i. e.*, he dreamed of home. Lived to be old. Called Thanksgiving 'Tom Kiver.'

## AN HOUR'S CONVERSATION

*April* 1, 1858.  When I started to walk that suddenly pleasant afternoon, the 28th of March, I crossed the path of the two brothers R., who were walking direct to the depot as if they had special business there that Sunday, the queer

short-legged dog running ahead. I talked with them an hour
there in the hope that the one who is not a stranger to me
would let something escape from his wise head. But he was
very moderate; all I got out of him to be remembered was
that in some town up-country where he lived when young,
they called the woodchuck 'squash-belly,' — with reference
to his form I suggested, but so far he had not advanced.
This he communicated very seriously, as an important piece
of information with which he labored. The other told me
how to raise a dog's dander, — any the gentlest dog's, —
by looking sternly in his face and making a peculiar sound
with your mouth. I then broke short the conference, continued my walk, while these gentlemen wheeled directly
about and walked straight back again.

### BOYS FISHING

*April* 6, 1858. Talked a moment with two little Irish (?)
boys, eight or ten years old, that were playing in the brook
by the mill. Saw one catch a minnow. I asked him if he
used a hook. He said no, it was a 'dully-chunk,' or some
such word. '*Dully* what?' [I] asked. 'Yes, *dully*,' said he,
and he would not venture to repeat the whole word again.
It was a small horsehair slip-noose at the end of a willow
stick four feet long. The horsehair was twisted two or three
together. He passed this over the fish slowly and then jerked
him out, the noose slipping and holding him. It seems they
are sometimes made with wire to catch trout. I asked him
to let me see the fish he had caught. It was a little pickerel
five inches long. . . . Asking what other fish he had caught, he
said a pike. 'That,' said I, 'is a large pickerel.' He said it had
'a long, long neb like a duck's bill.'

## A FISH TALK WITH WITHERELL

*May* 4, 1858. Coming back, I talk with Witherell at William Wheeler's landing. He comes pushing Wheeler's square-ended boat down-stream with a fish-spear. Says he caught a snapping turtle in the river May 1st. He sits on the side of my boat by the shore a little while, talking with me. There is a hole in the knee of his pants as big as your hand, and he keeps passing his hand over this slowly, to hide his bare skin, which is sunburnt and the color of his face, though the latter is reddened by rum, of which his breath smells. But how intimate he is with mud and its inhabitants! He says he caught a large pickerel the other night with spawn in it yet; that Henry Bigelow put many little trout into that round pond (Green Pond he calls it) on the Marlborough road, which Elbridge Haynes caught a few years after, weighing two or three pounds apiece. A man told him that he saw a trout weighing about a pound and a half darting at a pickerel, and every time he darted he took a bit off a fin, and at last the man walked in and caught the pickerel, and it weighed five pounds. This was in Spectacle Pond in Littleton. A fisherman told him once that the common eel 'gendered' into the river clam, and the young fed on the clam till they were big enough to get other food, and hence you found so many dead clams in the river. I asked him if he knew what fish made the stone-heaps in the river. He said the lamprey eel. He saw one making one last spring about this time, as he was going across the fields by the river near Tarbell's to get seed corn. It was a single lamprey piling up the stones. He used to see thousands of them where he lived a boy, where the lead pipe factory was.

### WEATHER PROPHETS

*August* 12, 1858. When I came down-stairs this morning, it raining hard and steadily, I found an Irishman sitting with his coat on his arm in the kitchen, waiting to see me. He wanted to inquire what I thought the weather would be to-day! I sometimes ask my aunt, and she consults the almanac. So we shirk the responsibility.

### A TALK WITH MINOTT

*August* 16, 1858. Talked with Minott, who sits in his wood-shed, having, as I notice, several seats there for visitors, — one a block on the sawhorse, another a patchwork mat on a wheelbarrow, etc., etc. His half-grown chickens, which roost overhead, perch on his shoulder or knee. According to him, the Holt is at the 'diving ash,' where is some of the deepest water in the river. He tells me some of his hunting stories again. He always lays a good deal of stress on the kind of gun he used, as if he had bought a new one every year, when probably he never had more than two or three in his life. In this case it was a 'half-stocked' one, a little 'cocking-piece,' and whenever he finished his game he used the word 'gavel,' I think in this way, 'gave him gavel,' *i. e.* made him bite the dust, or settled him. Speaking of foxes, he said: 'As soon as the nights get to be cool, if you step out-doors at nine or ten o'clock when all is still, you'll hear them bark out on the flat behind the houses, half a mile off, or sometimes *whistle* through their noses. I can tell 'em. I know what that means. I know all about that. They are out after something to eat, I suppose.' He used to love to hear the goldfinches sing on the hemp which grew near his gate.

## MINOTT ON SHATTUCK'S HISTORY

*August* 17, 1858.    Minott has only lately been reading Shattuck's 'History of Concord,' and he says that his account is not right by a jugful, that he does not come within half a mile of the truth, not as he has heard tell.

## EMERSON AS A SPORTSMAN

*August* 23, 1858.    Emerson says that he and Agassiz and Company broke some dozens of ale-bottles, one after another, with their bullets, in the Adirondack country, using them for marks! It sounds rather Cockneyish. He says that he shot a peetweet for Agassiz, and this, I think he said, was the first game he ever bagged. He carried a double-barrelled gun, — rifle and shotgun, — which he bought for the purpose, which he says received much commendation, — all parties thought it a very pretty piece. Think of Emerson shooting a peetweet (with shot) for Agassiz, and cracking an ale-bottle (after emptying it) with his rifle at six rods! They cut several pounds of lead out of the tree. It is just what Mike Saunders, the merchant's clerk, did when he was there.

### MINOTT ON MEADOW-HAYING

*August* 26, 1858.   Minott tells me that once, one very dry summer, when but part of these meadows had been cut, Moore and Hosmer got the owners to agree to have them burnt over, in the expectation that it would improve the quality of the grass, and they made quite an affair of it, — had a chowder, cooked by Moore's boys, etc.; but the consequence was that this wool-grass came in next year more than ever.

Some come a good way for their meadow-grass, even from Lincoln. George Baker has some in this meadow and some in the Sudbury meadows. But Minott says they want to get rid of their river meadow now, since they can get more and very much better grass off their redeemed swamps, or meadows of their own making, near home. Hardhack, meadow-sweet, alders, maples, etc., etc., appear to be creeping into the meadow. M. says they used to mow clean up to the ditch by the hard land. He remembers how he used to suffer from the heat, working out in the sun on these broad meadows, and when they took their luncheon, how glad he was to lie along close to the water, on the wet ground under the white maples by the riverside. And then one would swim a horse over at the Holt, go up to Jack Buttrick's (now Abner's), where there was a well of cool water, and get one or two great jugs full, with which he recrossed on the horse. He tells of one fellow who trod water across there with a jug in each hand!

### A HARD WORKER

*August* 29, 1858.   I hear A—— W—— complained of for overworking his cattle and hired men, but there is this to be said in his favor, that he does not spare himself.  They say that he made his horse 'Tom' draw twenty-nine hundred of hay to Boston the other day, — or night, — but then he put his shoulder to the wheel at every hill.  I hear that since then the horse has died, but W—— is alive and working.

### MINOTT AND BILLINGS'S DOG

*October* 18, 1858.   Minott was sitting outside, as usual, and inquired if I saw any game in my walks these days; since, now that he cannot go abroad himself, he likes to hear from the woods.  He tried to detain me to listen to some of his hunting-stories, especially about a slut that belonged to a neighbor by the name of Billings, which was excellent for squirrels, rabbits, and partridges, and would always follow him when he went out, though Billings was 'plaguy mad about it;' however, he had only to go by Billings's to have the dog accompany him.  B. afterward carried her up country and gave her away, the news of which almost broke Minott's heart.  He said he could have cried when he heard of it, for he had dreamed of her several nights.  She was a plaguy good dog for squirrels, etc., but her pups were none of them equal to herself.  It was not time for squirrels now, because the leaves were not off enough.  He used sometimes to take his old king's-arm on these excursions.  It was heavy, but it was sure. His present gun has a flint lock and has often heen repaired, and he said he didn't suppose it would fetch more than a dollar if put up at auction now. But he wouldn't take twenty dollars for it. He didn't want to part with it. He liked to look at it.

### THE CONCORD FISHERMEN

*October* 22, 1858. I see Heavy Haynes fishing in his old gray boat, sinking the stern deep. It is remarkable that, of the four fishermen who most frequent this river, — Melvin, Goodwin, and the two Hayneses, — the last three have all

been fishermen of the sea, have visited the Grand Banks, and are well acquainted with Cape Cod. These fishermen who sit thus alone from morning till night must be greater philosophers than the shoemakers.

### CHANNING AND THE RAIN

*November* 4, 1858.  A rainy day.

Called to C. from the outside of his house the other afternoon in the rain. At length he put his head out the attic window, and I inquired if he didn't want to take a walk, but he excused himself, saying that he had a cold. 'But,' added he, 'you can take so much the longer walk. Double it.'

### GOODWIN, THE ONE-EYED AJAX

*November* 4, 1858.  On the 1st, when I stood on Poplar Hill, I saw a man, far off by the edge of the river, splitting billets off a stump. Suspecting who it was, I took out my glass, and beheld Goodwin, the one-eyed Ajax, in his short blue frock, short and square-bodied, as broad as for his height he can afford to be, getting his winter's wood; for this is one of the phenomena of the season. As surely as the ants which he disturbs go into winter quarters in the stump when the weather becomes cool, so does G. revisit the stumpy shores with his axe. As usual, his powder-flask peeped out from a pocket on his breast, his gun was slanted over a stump near by, and his boat lay a little further along. He had been at work laying wall still further off, and now, near the end of the day, betook himself to those pursuits which he loved better still. It would be no amusement to me to see a gentleman buy his winter wood. It is to see G. get his. I helped him tip over a stump or two. He said that the owner of the land had given him leave to get them out, but it seemed to me a condescension for him to ask any man's leave to grub up these stumps. The stumps to those who can use them, I say, — to those who will split them. He might as well ask leave of the farmer to shoot the musquash and the meadow-hen, or I might as well ask leave to look at the landscape. Near by were large hollows in the ground, now grassed over, where he had got out white oak stumps in previous years. But, strange to say, the town does not like to have him get his fuel in this way. They would rather the stumps would rot in the ground, or be floated down-stream to the sea. They have almost without dissent agreed on a different mode of living, with their division of labor. They would have him stick to laying wall, and buy corded wood for his fuel, as they do. He has drawn up an old bridge sleeper and cut his name in it for security, and now he gets into his boat and pushes off in the twilight, saying he will go and see what Mr. Musquash is about.

### GUESSING AT AGES

*November* 6, 1858. I guessed at Goodwin's age on the 1st. He is hale and stout and looks younger than he is, and I took care to set him high enough. I guessed he was fifty-five, and he said that if he lived two or three months longer he would be fifty-six. He then guessed at my age, thought I was forty. He thought that Emerson was a very young-looking man for his age, 'But,' said he, 'he has not been out o' nights as much as you have.'

A SUICIDE

*November* 8, 1858. Goodwin, laying wall at Miss Ripley's, observed to me going by, 'Well, it seems that —— thought that he had lived long enough.' He committed suicide within a week, at his sister's house in Sudbury. A boy slept in the chamber with him, and, hearing a noise, got up and found —— on the floor with both his jugular veins cut, but his windpipe whole. He said to the boy, 'Take the razor and cut deeper,' but the boy ran, and —— died, and Garfield said it was about time, for ——, in revenge for being sent to the house of correction, had set fire to a pile of wood of his, that long pile by the roadside beyond William Wheeler's, that I stood under in a rain once. —— probably burned Witherell's house too, and perhaps Boynton's stable.

A WILD PIG

*November* 22, 1858. About the first of November a wild pig from the West, said to weigh three hundred pounds, jumped out of a car at the depot and made for the woods. The owner had to give up the chase at once, not to lose his passage, while some railroad employees pursued the pig even into the woods a mile and a half off, but there the pig turned and pursued them so resolutely that they ran for their lives and one climbed a tree. The next day being Sunday, they turned out in force with a gun and a large mastiff, but still the pig had the best of it, — fairly frightened the men by his fierce charges, — and the dog was so wearied and injured by the pig that the men were obliged to carry him in their arms. The pig stood it better than the dog. Ran between the gun man's legs, threw him over, and hurt his shoulder, though pierced in many places by a pitchfork. At the last accounts, he had been driven or baited into a barn in Lincoln, but no one durst enter, and they were preparing to shoot him. Such pork might be called venison.[1]

COOMBS'S HUNTING

*November* 28, 1858. I asked Coombs the other night if he had been a-hunting lately. He said he had not been out but once this fall. He went out the other day with a companion, and they came near getting a fox. They broke his leg. He has evidently been looking forward to some such success all summer. Having done thus much, he can afford to sit awhile by the stove at the post-office. He is plotting now how to break his head.

Goodwin cannot be a very bad man, he is so cheery.

[1] Caught him at last in a snare, and so conveyed him to Brighton. — H. D. T.

## MINOTT'S MEMORIES

*December* 18, 1858. Minott tells how he used to love to walk through swamps where great white pines grew and hear the wind sough in their tops. He recalls this now as he crouches over his stove, but he adds that it was dangerous, for even a small dead limb broken off by the wind and falling from such a height would kill a man at once.

## THE FARMER'S SINCERE LIFE

*December* 26, 1858. Call at a farmer's this Sunday afternoon, where I surprise the well-to-do masters of the house lounging in very ragged clothes (for which they think it necessary to apologize), and one of them is busy laying the supper-table (at which he invites me to sit down at last), bringing up cold meat from the cellar and a lump of butter on the end of his knife, and making the tea by the time his mother gets home from church. Thus sincere and homely, as I am glad to know, is the actual life of these New England men, wearing rags indoors there which would disgrace a beggar (and are not beggars and paupers they who *could be* disgraced so?) and doing the indispensable work, however humble. How much better and more humane it was than if they had imported and set up among their Penates a headless torso from the ruins of Ireland! I am glad to find that our New England life has a genuine humane core to it; that inside, after all, there is so little pretense and brag. Better than that, methinks, is the hard drinking and quarrelling which we must allow is not uncommon there. The middle-aged son sits there in the old unpainted house in a ragged coat, and helps his old mother about her work when the field does not demand him.

### THE PICKEREL-FISHER

*January* 19, 1859. A mile off I see the pickerel-fisher return-ing from the Holt, taking his way across the frozen meadows before sunset toward his hut on the distant bank. I know him (looking with my glass) by the axe over his shoulder, with his basket of fish and fish-lines hung on it, and the tin pail of minnows in his hand. The pail shines brightly more than a mile off, reflecting the setting sun. He starts early, knowing how quickly the sun goes down.

### THE MUSQUASH-HUNTERS

*January* 22, 1859. The musquash-hunter (last night), with his increased supply of powder and shot and boat turned up somewhere on the bank, now that the river is rapidly rising, dreaming of his exploits to-day in shooting musquash, of the great pile of dead rats that will weigh down his boat before night, when he will return wet and weary and weather-beaten to his hut with an appetite for his supper and for much slug-gish (punky) social intercourse with his fellows, — even he, dark, dull, and battered flint as he is, is an inspired man to his extent now, perhaps the most inspired by this freshet of any, and the Musketaquid Meadows cannot spare him. There are poets of all kinds and degrees, little known to each other. The Lake School is not the only or the principal one. They love various things. Some love beauty, and some love rum. Some go to Rome, and some go a-fishing, and are sent to the house of correction once a month. They keep up their fires by means unknown to me. I know not their comings and goings. How can I tell what violets they watch for? I know them wild and ready to risk all when their muse invites. The most sluggish will be up early enough then, and face any amount of wet and cold. I meet these gods of the river and woods with sparkling faces (like Apollo's) late from the house of correction, it may be carrying whatever mystic and forbidden bottles or other vessels concealed, while the dull regular priests are steering their parish rafts in a prose mood. What care I to see galleries full of representations of heathen gods, when I can see natural living ones by an infinitely superior artist, without perspective tube? If you read the Rig Veda, oldest of books, as it were, describing a very primitive people and condition of things, you hear in their prayers of a still older, more primitive and aboriginal race in their midst and round about, warring on them and seizing their flocks and herds, infesting their pastures. Thus is it in another sense in all communities, and hence the prisons and police.

I hear these guns going to-day, and I must confess they are to me a springlike and exhilarating sound, like the cock-crowing, though each one may report the death of a mus-quash. This, methinks, or the like of this, with whatever mixture of dross, is the real morning or evening hymn that goes up from these vales to-day, and which the stars echo. This is the best sort of glorifying of God and enjoying him that at all prevails here to-day, without any clarified butter or sacred ladles.

As a mother loves to see her child imbibe nourishment and expand, so God loves to see his children thrive on the nutriment he has furnished them. In the musquash-hunters I see the Almouchicois still pushing swiftly over the dark stream in their canoes. These aboriginal men cannot be repressed, but under some guise or other they survive and reappear continually. Just as simply as the crow picks up the worms which all over the fields have been washed out by the thaw, these men pick up the musquash that have been washed out the banks. And to serve such ends men plow and sail, and powder and shot are made, and the grocer exists to retail them, though he may think himself much more the deacon of some church.

### MILK-FARMING

*February* 25, 1859. Heard Staples, Tuttle, E. Wood, N. Barrett, and others this morning at the post-office talking about the profit of milk-farming. The general conclusion seemed to be that it was less profitable than it was three years ago. Yet Staples thought he could name half a dozen who had done well. He named one. He thought he could name eight or ten who had paid off the mortgages on their farms by this means within a few years. Tuttle said he would give him a good supper if he would name three. Staples named only the one referred to above, David Buttrick, but he added, looking at Tuttle, 'There is yourself. You know you came to town with nothing in your pocket but an old razor, a few pennies, and a damned dull jack-knife, and now you are richer than David Buttrick.' 'Well,' answered Tuttle, 'I shouldn't have been, if I hadn't used the razor so much.'

When it snowed yesterday very large flakes, an inch in diameter, Aunt said, 'They are picking geese.' This, it seems, is an old saying.

### HAIRWORK AND SPELLING

*March* 7, 1859. A lady tells me that she saw, last Cattle-Show Day, —— —— putting up a specimen of hairwork in a frame (by his niece) in the exhibition hall. I think it represented flowers, and underneath was written 'this Hare was taken from 8 different heads.' She made some sort of exclamation, betraying that there was some mistake in the writing, whereupon —— —— took it down and carried it off, but soon came back with a new description or label, 'this hare was taken from 8 different heads,' and thus it stood through the exhibition.

### UNCLE CHARLES'S EXPLOITS

*March* 11, 1859. E. Hosmer says that a man told him that he had seen my uncle Charles take a twelve-foot ladder, set it up straight, and then run up and down the other side, kicking it from behind him as he went down. E. H. told of seeing him often at the tavern toss his hat to the ceiling, twirling it over, and catch it on his head every time.

## GARFIELD'S TRAPPING

*March* 13, 1859. Talking with Garfield to-day about his trapping, he said that mink brought three dollars and a quarter, a remarkably high price, and asked if I had seen any. I said that I commonly saw two or three in a year. He said that he had not seen one alive for eight or ten years. 'But you trap them?' 'O yes,' he said. 'I catch thirty or forty dollars' worth every winter.' This suggests how little a trapper may see of his game. Garfield caught a skunk lately.

## THE EXCITEMENT OF A COLD DAY

*March* 19, 1859. While it is only moderately hot or cold, or wet or dry, nobody attends to it, but when Nature goes to an extreme in any of these directions we are all on the alert with excitement. Not that we care about the philosophy or the effects of this phenomenon. *E. g.*, when I went to Boston in the early train the coldest morning of last winter, two topics mainly occupied the attention of the passengers, Morphy's chess victories and Nature's victorious cold that morning. The inhabitants of various towns were comparing notes, and that one whose door opened upon a greater degree of cold than any of his neighbors' doors chuckled not a little. Almost every one I met asked me almost before our salutations were over 'how the glass stood' at my house or in my town, — the librarian of the college, the registrar of deeds at Cambridgeport, — a total stranger to me, whose form of inquiry made me think of another sort of glass, —

and each rubbed his hands with pretended horror but real delight if I named a higher figure than he had yet heard. It was plain that one object which the cold was given us for was our amusement, a passing excitement. It would be perfectly consistent and American to bet on the coldness of our respective towns, of [sic] the morning that is to come. Thus a greater degree of cold may be said to warm us more than a less one. We hear with ill-concealed disgust the figures reported from some localities, where they never enjoy the luxury of severe cold. This is a perfectly legitimate amusement, only we should know that each day is peculiar and has its kindred excitements.

### MUSQUASH AND MINK

*March* 25, 1859. A score of my townsmen have been shooting and trapping musquash and mink of late. Some have got nothing else to do. If they should strike for higher wages now, instead of going to the clam-banks, as the Lynn shoemakers propose, they would go to shooting musquash. They are gone all day; early and late they scan the rising tide; stealthily they set their traps in remote swamps, avoiding one another.

### PECUNIARY REWARD

*April* 3, 1859. Men's minds run so much on work and money that the mass instantly associate all literary labor with a pecuniary reward. They are mainly curious to know how much money the lecturer or author gets for his work. They think that the naturalist takes so much pains to collect plants or animals because he is paid for it. An Irishman who saw me in the fields making a minute in my note-book took it for granted that I was casting up my wages and actually inquired what they came to, as if he had never dreamed of any other use for writing. I might have quoted to him that the wages of sin is death, as the most pertinent answer. 'What do you get for lecturing now?' I am occasionally asked. It is the more amusing since I only lecture about once a year out of my native town, often not at all; so that I might as well, if my objects were merely pecuniary, give up the business. Once, when I was walking on Staten Island, looking about me as usual, a man who saw me would not believe me when I told him that I was indeed from New England but was not looking at that region with a pecuniary view, — a view to speculation; and he offered me a handsome bonus if I would sell his farm for him.

### STEDMAN BUTTRICK

*April* 18, 1859. When B. came to see me the other evening, and stood before the door in the dark, my mother asked, 'Who is it?' to which he replied, quite seriously, 'Lefttenant [*sic*] Stedman Buttrick.'

## TWO YOUNG FISHERMEN

*July* 31, 1859.   Stopped at Weir Hill Bend to cut a pole to sound with, and there came two real country boys to fish. One little fellow of seven or eight who talked like a man of eighty, — an old head, who had been, probably, brought up with old people. He was not willing to take up with my companion's jesting advice to bait the fish by casting in some of his worms, because, he said, 'It is too hard work to get them where we live.'

## SHOES AND THE WEARER

*September* 1, 1859.   Bought a pair of shoes the other day, and, observing that as usual they were only wooden-pegged at the toes, I required the seller to put in an extra row of iron pegs there while I waited for them. So he called to his boy to bring those zinc pegs, but I insisted on iron pegs and no zinc ones. He gave me considerable advice on the subject of shoes, but I suggested that even the wearer of shoes, of whom I was one, had an opportunity to learn some of their qualities. I have learned to respect my own opinion in this matter. As I do not use blacking and the seller often throws in a box of blacking when I buy a pair of shoes, they accumulate on my hands.

## A BAD DEBT

*September* 2, 1859.   I once did some surveying for a man who remarked, *but not till the job was done*, that he did not know when he should pay me. I did not pay much heed to this, though it was unusual, supposing that he meant to pay me some time or other. But after a while he sent to me a quart of red huckleberries, and this I thought was ominous and he distinguished me altogether too much by this gift, since I was not his particular friend. I saw it was the first installment, which would go a great way toward being the last. In course of years he paid a part of the debt in money, and that is the last I have heard of it.

## LYING

*September* 16, 1859.   When an Irishwoman tells me that she wouldn't tell a lie for her life (because I appear to doubt her), it seems to me that she has already told a lie. She holds herself and the truth very cheap to say that so easily.

## THE IDEAL AND THE REAL

*October* 3, 1859.   How all poets have idealized the farmer's life! What graceful figures and unworldly characters they have assigned to them! Serene as the sky, emulating nature with their calm and peaceful lives. As I come by a farmer's to-day, the house of one who died some two years ago, I see the decrepit form of one whom he had engaged to 'carry through,' taking his property at a venture, feebly tying up a bundle of fagots with his knee on it, though time is fast loosening the bundle that he is. When I look down on that roof I am not reminded of the mortgage which the village bank has on that property, — that that family long since sold itself to the devil and wrote the deed with their blood. I am not reminded that the old man I see in the yard is one who has lived beyond his calculated time, whom the young one is merely 'carrying through' in fulfillment of his contract; that the man at the pump is watering the milk. I am not reminded of the idiot that sits by the kitchen fire.

### CHECKERBERRY-TEA

*November* 28, 1859. Goodwin tells me that Therien, who lives in a shanty of his own building and alone in Lincoln, uses for a drink only checkerberry-tea. (G. also called it 'ivory-leaf.') Is it not singular that probably only one *tea*-drinker in this neighborhood should use for his beverage a plant which grows here? Therien, really drinking his checkerberry-tea from motives of simplicity or economy and saying nothing about it, deserves well of his country. As he does now, we may all do at last.

## A BASKET OF CHIPS

*November* 28, 1859.  Saw Abel Brooks there with a half-bushel basket on his arm.  He was picking up chips on his and neighboring lots; had got about two quarts of old and blackened pine chips, and with these was returning home at dusk more than a mile.  Such a petty quantity as you would hardly have gone to the end of your yard for, and yet he said that he had got more than two cords of them at home, which he had collected thus and sometimes with a wheelbarrow.  He had thus spent an hour or two and walked two or three miles in a cool November evening to pick up two quarts of pine chips scattered through the woods.  He evidently takes real satisfaction in collecting his fuel, perhaps

gets more heat of all kinds out of it than any man in town. He is not reduced to taking a walk for exercise as some are. It is one thing to *own* a wood-lot as he does who perambulates its bounds almost daily, so as to have worn a path about it, and another to own one as many another does who hardly knows where it is. Evidently the quantity of chips in his basket is not essential; it is the chippy idea which he pursues. It is to him an unaccountably pleasing occupation. And no doubt he loves to see his pile grow at home.

Think how variously men spend the same hour in the same village! The lawyer sits talking with his client in the twilight; the trader is weighing sugar and salt; while Abel Brooks is hastening home from the woods with his basket half full of chips. I think I should prefer to be with Brooks. He was literally as smiling as a basket of chips. A basket of chips, therefore, must have been regarded as a singularly pleasing (if not pleased) object.

### ONE OF JOHN BROWN'S MEN

*December* 3, 1859. Rode with a man this forenoon who said that if he did not clean his teeth when he got up, it made him sick all the rest of the day, but he had found by late experience that when he had not cleaned his teeth for several days they cleaned themselves. I assured him that such was the general rule, — that when from any cause we were prevented from doing what we had commonly thought indispensable for us to do, things *cleaned* or took care of themselves.

X [1] was betrayed by his eyes, which had a glaring film over

[1] X, whom Thoreau drove this morning to Acton, was literally an unknown quantity to him at the time. He did not learn till afterward that it was Francis Jackson Merriam, one of John Brown's men, on his way to Canada.

them and no serene depth into which you could look. Inquired particularly the way to Emerson's and the distance, and when I told him, said he knew it as well as if he saw it. Wished to turn and proceed to his house. Told me one or two things which he asked me not to tell S.[1] Said, 'I know I am insane,' — and I knew it too. Also called it 'nervous excitement.' At length, when I made a certain remark, he said, 'I don't know but *you* are Emerson; are you? You look somewhat like him.' He said as much two or three times, and added once, 'But then Emerson wouldn't lie.' Finally put his questions to me, of Fate, etc., etc., as if I *were* Emerson. Getting to the woods, I remarked upon them, and he mentioned my name, but never to the end suspected who his companion was. Then 'proceeded to business,' — 'since the time was short,' — and put to me the questions he was going to put to Emerson. His insanity exhibited itself chiefly by his incessant excited talk, scarcely allowing me to interrupt him, but once or twice apologizing for his behavior. What he said was for the most part connected and sensible enough.

CHANNING PREFERS THE ROAD

*December* 22, 1859.  C. is inclined to walk in the road, it being better walking there, and says: 'You don't wish to see anything but the sky to-day and breathe this air. You could walk in the city to-day, just as well as in the country. You only wish to be out.' This was because I inclined to walk in the woods or by the river.

[1] Mr. F. B. Sanborn.

## A CREATURE OF FATE

*January* 9, 1860. I hear that R. M——, a rich old farmer who lives in a large house, with a male housekeeper and no other family, gets up at three or four o'clock these winter mornings and milks seventeen cows regularly. When asked why he works so hard he answers that the poor are obliged to work hard. Only think, what a creature of fate he is, this old Jotun, milking his seventeen cows though the thermometer goes down to −25°, and not knowing why he does it, — draining sixty-eight cows' teats in the dark of the coldest morning! Think how helpless a rich man who can only do as he has done, and as his neighbors do, one or all of them! What an account he will have to give of himself! He spent some time in a world, alternately cold and warm, and every winter morning, with lantern in hand, when the frost goblins were playing their tricks, he resolutely accomplished his task and milked his seventeen cows, while the man housekeeper prepared his breakfast! If this were original with him, he would be a hero to be celebrated in history. Think how tenaciously every man does his deed, of some kind or other, though it be idleness! He is rich, dependent on nobody, and nobody is dependent on him; has as good health as the average, at least, can do as he pleases, as we say. Yet he gravely rises every morning by candle-light, dons his cowhide boots and his frock, takes his lantern and wends to the barn and milks his seventeen cows, milking with one hand while he warms the other against the cow or his person. This is but the beginning of his day, and his Augean stable work. So serious is the life he lives.

## A BUSHEL OF NUTMEGS

*January* 13, 1860.   Tuttle was saying to-day that he did remember a certain man's living with him once, from something that occurred. It was this: The man was about starting for Boston market for Tuttle, and Mrs. Tuttle had been telling him what to get for her. The man inquired if that was all, and Mrs. Tuttle said no, she wanted some nutmegs. 'How many,' he asked. Tuttle, coming along just then, said, 'Get a bushel.' When the man came home he said that he had had a good deal of trouble about the nutmegs. He could not find so many as were wanted, and, besides, they told him that they did not sell them by the bushel. But he said that he would take a bushel by the weight. Finally he made out to get a peck of them, which he brought home. It chanced that nutmegs were very high just then, so Tuttle, after selecting a few for his own use, brought the remainder up to town and succeeded in disposing of them at the stores for just what he gave for them.

## INDIVIDUALITY IN GAIT

*February* 5, 1860.   Coming home last night in the twilight, I recognized a neighbor a dozen rods off by his walk or carriage, though it was so dark that I could not see a single feature of his person. Indeed, his person was all covered up excepting his face and hands, and I could not possibly have distinguished these at this distance from another man's. Nor was it owing to any peculiarity in his dress, for

I should have known him though he had had on a perfectly new suit. It was because the man within the clothes moved them in a peculiar manner that I knew him thus at once at a distance and in the twilight. He made a certain figure in any clothes he might wear, and moved in it in a peculiar manner. Indeed, we have a very intimate knowledge of one another; we see through thick and thin; spirit meets spirit. A man hangs out innumerable signs by which we may know him. So, last summer, I knew another neighbor half a mile off up the river, though I did not see him, by the manner in which the breath from his lungs and mouth, *i. e.* his voice, made the air strike my ear. In that manner he communicated himself to all his acquaintance within a diameter of one mile (if it were all up and down the river). So I remember to have been sure once in a very dark night who was preceding me on the sidewalk, — though I could not see him, — by the sound of his tread. I was surprised to find that I knew it.

And to-day, seeing a peculiar very long track of a man in the snow, who had been along up the river this morning, I guessed that it was George Melvin, because it was accompanied by a hound's track. There was a thin snow on the ice, and I observed that he not only furrowed the snow for a foot before he completed his step, but that the toe of his track was always indefinite, as if his boot had been worn out and prolonged at the toe. I noticed that I and my companion made a clear and distinct track at the toe, but when I experimented, and tried to make a track like this by not lifting my feet but gliding and partly scuffing along, I found myself walking just like Melvin, and that perfectly convinced me that it was he.[1]

We have no occasion to wonder at the instinct of a dog.

[1] I told him of it afterward, and he gave a corresponding account of himself. — H. D. T.

In these last two instances I surpassed the instinct of the dog.

It may always be a question how much or how little of a man goes to any particular act. It is not merely by taking time and by a conscious effort that he betrays himself. A man is revealed, and a man is concealed, in a myriad unexpected ways; *e. g.*, I can hardly think of a more effectual way of disguising neighbors to one another than by stripping them naked.

### A WOODCHUCK-SKIN CAP

*February* 28, 1860.   Passed a very little boy in the street to-day, who had on a home-made cap of a woodchuck-skin, which his father or elder brother had killed and cured, and his mother or elder sister had fashioned into a nice warm cap. I was interested by the sight of it, it suggested so much of family history, adventure with the chuck, story told about it, not without exaggeration, the human parents' care of their young these hard times. Johnny was promised many times, and now the work has been completed, — a perfect little idyl, as they say. The cap was large and round, big enough, you would say, for the boy's father, and had some kind of cloth visor stitched to it. The top of the cap was evidently the back of the woodchuck, as it were expanded in breadth, contracted in length, and it was as fresh and handsome as if the woodchuck wore it himself. The great gray-tipped wind hairs were all preserved, and stood out above the brown only a little more loosely than in life. As if he put his head into the belly of a woodchuck, having cut off his tail and legs and substituted a visor for

## PLATE X

*Johnny and his Woodchuck-Skin Cap*

the head. The little fellow wore it innocently enough, not knowing what he had on, forsooth, going about his small business pit-a-pat; and his black eyes sparkled beneath it when I remarked on its warmth, even as the woodchuck's might have done. Such should be the history of every piece of clothing that we wear.

## COUNTRY LIFE IN LINCOLN

*February* 28, 1860. I hear this account of Austin: —

An acquaintance who had bought him a place in Lincoln took him out one day to see it, and Austin was so smitten with the quiet and retirement and other rural charms that he at once sold his house in Concord, bought a small piece of rocky pasture in an out-of-the-way part of this out-of-the-way town, and with the funds raised by the sale of his

old house built him a costly stone house upon it. Now he
finds that this retirement (or country life) is the very thing
which he does not want, but, his property being chiefly
invested in the house, he is caught in a trap, as it were,
for he cannot sell it, though he advertises it every year. As
for society, he has none; his neighbors are few and far between, and he never visits them nor they him. They can
do without him, being old settlers, *adscripti glebae*. He
found one man in the next town who got his living by
sporting and fishing, and he has built him a little hut and
got him to live on his place for society and helpfulness. He
cannot get help either for the outdoor or indoor work.
There are none thereabouts who work by the day or job,
and servant-girls decline to come so far into the country.
Surrounded by grain-fields, he sends to Cambridge for his
oats, and, as for milk, he can scarcely get any at all, for the
farmers all send it to Boston, but he has persuaded one to
leave some for him at the depot half a mile off.

### AN IRISHMAN'S FUEL

*February* 28, 1860.   As I go down the Boston road, I see an
Irishman wheeling home from far a large damp and rotten
pine log for fuel. He evidently sweats at it, and pauses to
rest many times. He found, perhaps, that his wood-pile
was gone before the winter was, and he trusts thus to contend with the remaining cold. I see him unload it in his
yard before me and then rest himself. The piles of solid
oak wood which I see in other yards do not interest me at
all, but this looked like *fuel*. It warmed me to think of it.
He will now proceed to split it finely, and then I fear it will

require almost as much heat to dry it as it will give out at last. How rarely we are encouraged by the sight of simple actions in the street! We deal with banks and other institutions, where the life and humanity are concealed, — what there is. I like at least to see the great beams half exposed in the ceiling or the corner.

## THE WALKER'S CLOTHES

*March* 26, 1860. C. was saying, properly enough, the other day, as we were making our way through a dense patch of shrub oak: 'I suppose that those villagers think that we wear these old and worn hats with holes all along the corners for oddity, but Coombs, the musquash-hunter and partridge and rabbit snarer, knows better. He understands us. He knows that a new and square-cornered hat would be spoiled in one excursion through the shrub oaks.'

The walker and naturalist does not wear a hat, or a shoe, or a coat, to be looked at, but for other uses. When a citizen comes to take a walk with me I commonly find that he is lame, — disabled by his shoeing. He is sure to wet his feet, tear his coat, and jam his hat, and the superior qualities of my boots, coat, and hat appear. I once went into the woods with a party for a fortnight. I wore my old and common clothes, which were of Vermont gray. They wore, no doubt, the best they had for such an occasion, — of a fashionable color and quality. I thought that they were a little ashamed of me while we were in the towns. They all tore their clothes badly but myself, and I, who, it chanced, was the only one provided with needles and thread, enabled them to mend them. When we came out of the woods I was the best dressed of any of them.

## HUMAN VERMIN

*May* 2, 1860.   A crowd of men seem to generate vermin even of the human kind.  In great towns there is degradation undreamed of elsewhere, — gamblers, dog-killers, rag-pickers.  Some live by robbery or by luck.  There was the Concord muster (of last September).  I see still a well-dressed man carefully and methodically searching for money on the muster-fields, far off across the river.  I turn my glass upon him and notice how he proceeds.  (I saw them searching there in the fall till the snow came.)  He walks regularly and slowly back and forth over the ground where the soldiers had their tents, — still marked by the straw, — with his head prone, and poking in the straw with a stick, now and then turning back or aside to examine something more closely.  He is dressed, methinks, better than an average man whom you meet in the streets.  How can he pay for his board thus.  He dreams of finding a few coppers, or perchance a half-dime, which have fallen from the soldiers' pockets, and no doubt he *will* find something of the kind, having dreamed of it, — having knocked, this door will be opened to him.

## MOUNT MONADNOCK

*August* 9, 1860.   There were a great many visitors to the summit, both by the south and north, *i. e.* the Jaffrey and Dublin paths, but they did not turn off from the beaten track.  One noon, when I was on the top, I counted forty men, women, and children around me, and more were con-

stantly arriving while others were going. Certainly more
than one hundred ascended in a day. When you got within
thirty rods you saw them seated in a row along the gray
parapets, like the inhabitants of a castle on a gala-day; and
when you behold Monadnock's blue summit fifty miles off
in the horizon, you may imagine it covered with men, women,
and children in dresses of all colors, like an observatory on a
muster-field. They appeared to be chiefly mechanics and
farmers' boys and girls from the neighboring towns. The
young men sat in rows with their legs dangling over the
precipice, squinting through spy-glasses and shouting and
hallooing to each new party that issued from the woods
below. Some were playing cards; others were trying to see
their house or their neighbor's. Children were running
about and playing as usual. Indeed, this peak in pleasant
weather is the most trivial place in New England. There
are probably more arrivals daily than at any of the White
Mountain houses. Several were busily engraving their
names on the rocks with cold-chisels, whose incessant clink
you heard, and they had but little leisure to look off. The
mountain was not free of them from sunrise to sunset,
though most of them left about 5 P. M. At almost any hour
of the day they were seen wending their way single file in
various garb up or down the shelving rocks of the peak.
These figures on the summit, seen in relief against the sky
(from our camp), looked taller than life. I saw some that
camped there, by moonlight, one night. On Sunday,
twenty or thirty at least, in addition to the visitors to the
peak, came up to pick blueberries, and we heard on all
sides the rattling of dishes and their frequent calls to each
other.

A SHREWD DEACON

*March* 8, 1861.   A lady tells me that she met Deacon S. of Lincoln with a load of hay, and she, noticing that as he drove under the apple trees by the side of the road a considerable part of the hay was raked off by their boughs, informed him of it.   But he answered, 'It is not mine yet. I am going to the scales with it and intend to come back this way.'

# Index

# INDEX